Any Minute Now

David Meldrum

Any Minute Now

Any Minute Now
ISBN 978 1 76041 879 3
Copyright © David Meldrum 2020

First published 2020 by
GINNINDERRA PRESS
PO Box 3461 Port Adelaide 5015
www.ginninderrapress.com.au

Contents

Part One: Adolescence

A Bad Reputation	13
Corny Point	18
The Shotgun	24
Mr Hopper	28
Two Caterpillars In the Desert	31
A Very Slow Degree	42
Being Brave	46
Sergeant Pepper's Lonely Hearts Club Band	50
Bad Taxi Fare	52

Part Two: A Young Careerist

The Swimming Club Minutes Secretary	57
The Hill	63
Robert	72
A Very Silly Risk	76
Dudley Brown	80
Beating the Odds	84
16 February 1983 – *The Age* Newspaper	88
No Spilt Milk	97

Part Three: So Many Adventures

A Little Piece of Mental Health Services Reform	107
A Few Seconds Left	120
Oak Valley	126
All That Jazz	132
Not a Fokker Friendship	141

Bad Job Choice	147
Teeth At Risk	153
Up In Flames	159
Whatever It Takes	164
My Focus Is Mental Illness	173
Retirement	187

Prologue

A few years ago, I was on the board of a community body that focused on improving health services outside hospitals. We made a costly error from the start, by not recruiting enough local member organisations. The one we did have was a GP-led group, which we could see was becoming unhappy with some of our policies. When we looked closely at our constitution, we realised they could just vote us out, so we scrambled and found three more potential members. We met one evening to approve them joining, but it was too late. Our CEO arrived at the office to find the doors padlocked. Our one member had sacked us.

Next morning, one of my fellow board members rang me. He was furious. 'David, this is a disgraceful situation. We're a pretty solid bunch of citizens.' (I assume he meant we had important jobs and so on.) 'They can't do this to us.'

I said, 'Well, they just have. I live with the thought that any minute now they're going to be on to me. It's happened again. I guess it's time to get together and work out what to do now.'

When I put the phone down, I sat and reflected. 'Any minute now. There's a recurring theme in my life. If I ever get around to a memoir, I might use it for the title.'

Most of the material in this book came to me randomly; in remembered episodes from my past that I posted on my blog. Until recently, I had no plan to make any sort of narrative arc from it all. At first it was one story every week or two, interspersed with jottings about all manner of topical issues, but soon I found I was thinking every day about my childhood, about jobs I had had, people I could remember.

Whole paragraphs formed in my head. Chance comments or scenes in books or movies would set me off, and I know I started to be even more guilty of zoning out than usual.

There was no clear chronology – memories hit me from last year, from more than fifty years ago, in no order. I made no notes. A story would take shape in my thinking, and one day I would just sit down and write for a few hours. Of course, I polished sentences, changed a phrase here and there, and debated spelling with Microsoft, but these contents are just about as they blurted out of my mind, through to my fingers on the keyboard.

The experience was sometimes emotionally exhausting, but always exhilarating, driven by a compulsion to get the events, the people, and even some of the inner world of my mind down on paper. The next compulsion was to get a comment on the work – from my partner Charmaine first, then a few friends. The idea of a blog had appealed without warning – it was something about being accountable for this version of my history, saying to anybody who was interested, 'Well, this is how I remember it.' When you press that 'publish now' button, it's a giddy feeling, a bit like sending off a job application; only I'm not asking for anything, except perhaps for attentive readers; hoping I've delivered some entertaining moments. To my tiny handful of responding blog readers, a big thank you; you're an important part of why I kept writing.

By the time I had more than 50,000 words of memoir bits out there, I knew I wanted to try something daunting – to put it all down more or less chronologically, partly to see if there was any discernible process of maturing, of learning something useful about life, of moving towards fulfilment, that might emerge from the constant fog of daily events. Once I made that decision, I had to write an outline, a plan, and it showed me where there were whole chunks of my life missing, times past that had not been front of mind when I was blogging.

Some of those gaps filled themselves in easily – many more memories, good and bad, seemed impatient to become prose. Others involved a struggle to be honest, especially the first story about my delinquent youth. And, I guess, like any memoirist I had to set limits: there's only so much that can or should spill on to a public page. In my case, that lead me to write a lot about my work life, but not much about family and other personal relationships, at least as they developed after my adolescence. Work has been hugely important to me; perhaps more so than for most people I know. It may be in work that I found the confidence that had escaped me as an adolescent; giving me endless opportunities to prove myself. But I still know it's nowhere near the whole story, of mine or any other life. I think it's just the way this writing process turned out.

I've read it all a few times, and talked about it with my partner Charmaine, trying to get a sense of the whole. I think it's more like a French movie than a Hollywood one, with few certainties, more than a few moral ambiguities, and some very mixed outcomes. If any big meanings jump out at you, please let me know. The recurring patterns of my work, the things that give me joy and occasionally despair, and the possible outcomes of some events in my youth – all of these just refuse to add up to a simple tale of orderly development. My one hope is that you find it a good read.

Part One

Adolescence

A Bad Reputation

If adolescence marks the beginning of a clearer sense of who you are, with inklings of who you do and don't want to be, I hit it at twelve years old when a girl told me I had a bad reputation.

For the previous three or four years, I had been a very naughty boy – not all the time of course, but often enough to be a worry to my parents. And they didn't know half of the things I got up to, often with my younger brother as a willing accomplice. Shoplifting was my debut, after a friend in school told me he had grabbed some fireworks from the newsagency. I had the perfect accessory – a double-breasted overcoat with big two-way pockets – so it was easy to lean over an item and slip it in without appearing to put your hands near the merchandise. I was spotted first time.

The next day, Dad confronted me, telling me I had been seen hovering near some toys, and now they were missing. I confessed immediately, knowing I had no choice, and Dad returned the toys. Apart from being grounded and losing my pocket money for a month or so, I can't recall any other punishments that hurt much. Dad rarely hit us, but I was worried about the school principal finding out, because he was very free with the cane. That didn't happen, and I wouldn't understand until years later that it was my dad's intervention that literally saved my arse.

After maybe a year of limiting my risky impulses to standard boys' stuff, like destroying ants' nests, stone-throwing fights and scaring the neighbour's cows, my next crime was putting objects on the railway line near our house. At first it was just pennies and small metal toys, with pleasing results. But I wanted to see what would happen if we put a large thing in front of the huge steam train that came through late most evenings, filling the valley with noise and smoke. We found just the right choice near the tracks; an empty, rusty forty-four-gallon drum. As soon it was dark, we snuck out of the house and put the barrel on the track.

My brother and I shared a bedroom, and we peered out into the darkness when we heard the long, mournful train whistle. Suddenly I was terrified, realising this was going way too far, and an awful accident might be about to happen. I just hoped the barrel would be crunched flat, and wouldn't cause a derailment or worse. But that night the train slowed right down, coming to a stop at the station, and we assumed it had bunted the barrel to the side. But the next morning we couldn't find it, and for a long time afterwards I feared the knock on the door asking if we boys, who were often seen playing near the tracks, were responsible for a very serious crime. In fact, no one seemed to know about the barrel. Nobody said anything, so we just swore a vow of silence on the whole matter.

Over the next few years, among other exploits, my brother and I vandalised street lights, made guns out of pipes and firecrackers and stole money and cigarettes from our parents. One of the worst was partly an accident. Dad and my brothers, along with his friend Ian and two of his sons, went camping next to the River Murray. While Dad and Ian went into town to get drunk as usual, I looked in Ian's car and found a rifle. I played with it for a while, pointing at birds in trees and imaginary rabbits in the grass. I stopped to speak to my brother, holding the gun in front of me, and for some reason pulled the trigger. There was a sharp crack, and a hole appeared in Ian's car door. He had left his .22 rifle loaded and cocked, which doesn't make it his fault, but was a very stupid thing for an experienced shooter to do.

Unsurprisingly, the other boys distanced themselves from my problem immediately. I opened the door and found no hole on the other side. The bullet must have been inside the door, probably sitting at the bottom. The car was very untidy, and mud-spattered, so I decided to try disguising the damage by throwing new mud along the side, after plugging the hole with mud also. It looked quite convincing, but I knew it would dry out, and then most likely fall out at the first big bump on the rough dirt tracks. My chances seemed slim. The other boys kept the secret, Ian's sons probably because of his famous temper, and my brothers through loyalty.

Again, there were no consequences. While I waited for the axe to fall, Ian drove that car around Mount Barker, my home town, for months afterwards, with the mud untouched. He often came to our house, and parked right in front of where we would sit and eat from the family barbecue, with the door facing us. About a year later, I saw him driving a new car. I never knew when or if Ian or the new owner discovered the bullet hole, or if Ian ever harboured any suspicions.

When I turned twelve, my best birthday present was a pocket knife. Typing now, I can still see the scar on my knuckle where I accidentally closed it on my index finger. Of course, I tried cutting everything I could find – plants, ropes, wood and so on – but I still don't understand what I was thinking when I took to the hoses on my neighbour's milking machine. I can see them now – red rubber that my knife whipped through so easily. The next evening, having forgotten about the hoses completely, I felt no fear when I answered the door to the local police sergeant. There was no one else at home, but that didn't stop him questioning me. I was a pushover.

'Hello, there. David, isn't it? Tell me, David, have you got a sharp pocket knife?'

I couldn't wait to pull it out of my pocket to show him.

'A very smart little number. So, what would you know about the rubber hoses on the milking machine next door – the ones that I reckon have been cut by a knife just like yours?'

I was dumbstruck, and very afraid.

He pressed on. 'It was you, wasn't it, David? I think we need to have a talk with your father about what to do. Your neighbour is pressing me to take legal action.'

My silent tears were my confession.

Perhaps at that moment he realised he was overstepping the mark, questioning a twelve-year-old alone at night, because he said, 'I'll be talking to your father about this in the morning. And I'll have that knife now, please.' Leaving me alone in a state of panic.

Yet again I got off lightly, at least in the short term. I was taken by Dad to give a shame-faced apology to a furious neighbour, Dad paid for the hoses to be replaced, and no charges were laid. Dad told me to say nothing about the matter to anyone, and I didn't. But Dad did say to me that he had great difficulty in talking our neighbour out of legal action, and he just hoped other people in our little town didn't find out. I was never afraid of my father, but his obvious disappointment cut me deeply. Completely self-absorbed, it never occurred to me how much this and my previous shoplifting might have cost him in his social standing. As one of the big bosses in Mount Barker, he could call in favours, but this one must have hurt.

I might have gone on to more juvenile crime, but for two things. The first was when a boy in my class, from one of the poorest families in the district, was sent to a reform school for a year. I think he stole some money from a neighbour. I stopped to think about a couple of others who had gone before him. It hit me that I only got off because Dad was well-off and influential. It just didn't feel right. But the cruncher was all about a girl. She lived not far from our place, and I had a crush on her, with absolutely no way to express that.

One day I saw her walking home in front of me, and I joined her, offering to carry her bag.

She looked at me, not unkindly, and said, 'I'm not allowed to talk to you David, because my parents say you have a bad reputation.'

I couldn't think of anything useful to say, so we walked along in silence until we got to her gate.

'Goodbye, David.'

I went home in tears. The thought that other people, especially the girl I was swooning over, saw me like that was just about unbearable. How many people knew? Did Mum and Dad know people were talking? The girl never spoke to me again, and I tried to avoid her whenever possible.

And from that day on, I have never stolen anything or vandalised property. I spent the rest of my adolescence fully aware of how close I went to ruining my life, which only added to my general lack of self-confidence. As an adult, I've found other ways to be thoughtless, to be careless about the rights of others and to take stupid risks. But my urge to do something destructive, just for the sake of it, went away when a girl taught me a little about the wages of sin.

Corny Point

Over our evening meal, Dad told us one of his workmates had invited us to spend our Christmas holidays in his friend's old farmhouse at Corny Point, on Yorke Peninsula. I think it was 1958, and the year before we had been on Kangaroo Island, one of the almost mythical memories of my boyhood. I caught my first fish there, on a green string line, followed improbably by a small shark. It still rankles that my school friends said I was bullshitting about the shark, when I'd thought I'd be the star of 'what I did in the holidays' morning talks. Not for the last time, my tendency to be caught out exaggerating had cost me an authentic opportunity for glory

Dad said Corny Point was going to be even better than the island, with a great ocean beach, lots of fish to catch, and swimming and snorkelling opportunities galore. All of us were going, even my older brother Hamish, who at sixteen was starting to rebel against most involvement with the family. He only agreed to come when Dad allowed him to buy a speargun. We bought fishing reels, lines, hooks and sinkers, our first Esky for keeping Dad's Coopers Ale and Mum's Seppelts dry sherry cold, and set about packing our brand-new Holden Special station wagon to the hilt. That car had the full plastic seat covers so popular at the time, which were excruciatingly uncomfort- able in the heatwave conditions. 'To keep the seats like new for when you come to sell the car' was the refrain. Of course, the next owners kept them on too, so generations of drivers and passengers endured sweaty legs and backs, while they slipped around on the bench seats at every corner.

The trip took nearly four hours, without air conditioning, and we had to stop several times to get cold drinks and icy poles. The radio was a slight distraction, but Mum and Dad preferred the ABC, so it was all news, earnest discussions and classical music, rather than the rock and roll that Hamish wanted. He was deeply into Little Richard, Chuck Berry and the soon-to-be dead Buddy Holly, and spent most of his money on the 45rpm EPs that brought new music within budget reach of teenagers. Singers such as those cut no ice with the ABC in those days – Triple J was thirty years away.

The last hour was on a very rough, corrugated dirt road, the car throwing up clouds of dust across the yellow-beige barley fields. Huge flocks of pink and grey galahs rose from the ground when we came near. Predictably, when an occasional car came the other way, we got their dust through every loose seal and vent; it got into our mouths, our eyes and of course all our gear packed in the rear. With the temperature hovering near forty degrees Centigrade, five tired and very grumpy people eventually pulled up beside the Corny Point General Store, with its one hand-operated petrol pump. The older man who came out to serve us wore a long-sleeved shirt, thick wool trousers held up by braces and big leather boots. We three boys, in T-shirts, shorts and thongs, couldn't understand anyone being that stupid in this heat.

With detailed directions from him, we found the farmhouse. It was love at first sight, at least for us boys. The house had been empty for a decade or more, the family having moved a few hundred metres to a new place with such wonders as electricity, running water and an inside toilet. Built in stages between 1850 and 1880, the walls and floors of the old house consisted of huge limestone blocks, cut from the ground around it, with doors and window frames rough-hewn from trees nearby. I'm not sure how they did the original roof, but by the 1870s, corrugated iron was coming from England and Europe, used as ballast in the magnificent sailing clippers that then loaded wheat and barley for the return trip to Europe. In the kitchen, a handmade table with benches sat beside a wood stove that became the focal point of many happy nights to come. From the front doorstep, just across a barley paddock, the sea beckoned.

As we began unpacking, an old Chevrolet (1938, I think) approached from the direction of the new house. The car was so dirty and dusty it was almost perfectly camouflaged on its home ground. The door creaked open and out got the owner of the property, Jack Barclay. Again, the thick pants and braces, and a khaki shirt, but this time topped with a weathered wide-brimmed hat. We found out later that Jack was seventy-eight, and had been born in the house we were going to use. After saying hello, he invited Dad, just Dad, to come back to his place for a cold beer. Dad getting drunk with Jack became a several-times-weekly occurrence. None of us liked this, because Dad would return in an unhelpful and sometimes surly state. He would be dropped off by Jack from his car, which he was driving almost dead-drunk, but on his own land and so within the law, if not common sense. One day, he misjudged the approach and stopped by running into a stone shed outside our gate. When we went to investigate, Jack was asleep at the wheel.

But we boys, if not so much Mum at first, were in paradise. Mum was facing challenges such as how to keep food in that heat without a fridge, or even fly-proof cupboards. Meanwhile, Hamish found the drop toilet – a hole in the ground about three metres deep, in which we could see redback spider webs. Great for speeding up the process and so daring. It became a little too exciting when one of us – I think it was Hamish – sat down and closed the door, to find a brown snake curled up behind it. He did the only thing he could, waiting in fear until it slowly disappeared under the door and back to the paddocks.

We explored the adjoining workshop, which was completely equipped up to pre-World War II standards, with no electricity. Millstone sharpeners, adzes, a forge, bellows, and endless small tools like augers and handsaws. We happily sharpened knives, lit the forge to make iron horseshoes glow red, and bored holes in pieces of wood. In our enthusiasm, we didn't put things back where we found them, and Jack came over a couple of days later to fit a big padlock to the workshop. It would be twenty years or more, with tools of my own, and children, before I properly understood his point of view.

On day two, we went as directed to West Beach (or Berry Bay on some maps) to look for 'Pearl's pool'. Pearl was Jack's wife, still at home at that time, but with early signs of the dementia that would see her in a nursing home within a year or two. The pool was so named because Pearl used to go swimming there, in the nude, with all farmhands under strict instructions to keep away from the adjoining beach. We parked the car, and walked up through sandhills, emerging to a view that has stopped me in my tracks ever since. I feel a rush of nostalgia as I write this, hearing the crash of the waves, and seeing the huge sweep of the bay and the ocean. It was and still remains one of those places and moments when you are blissfully insignificant in the face of endless beauty. Below us, surrounded but completely protected from a tremendous surf, Pearl's pool twinkled, emerald green laced with white water from waves splashing high from the rocks.

The pool is about fifty metres by thirty, and a couple of metres deep in the centre. We soon found that by daring to sit on the seaward rocks, we could be lifted bodily by the spray of a big wave, thrown into the air and into the pool. It was dangerous of course; slip, and the rocks were very sharp on the legs and back, as a few of our more tentative guests found out over the years. In the pool, schools of small fished cruised close to us, and abalone beckoned from the underside of the rocks. We learnt how to remove them with a sharp knife, and how to tenderise them before cooking. The meat is delicious, and the cleaned shells are great ornaments. I re-experienced those days recently when I found a small abalone shell on a local beach. Actually, it was the moment that decided me to write this.

At one side of the pool, there was a rock platform where Dad and we three boys could throw a line into the surf. It was a dicey spot, with the biggest waves swirling around our ankles. It takes nerve to watch a four-metre monster wave loom up to crash against the reef just in front of you, hoping this won't be the freak one that knocks you off the rocks. But the fishing was so good we couldn't resist. Sometimes we needed more bait, and the limpets on the rocks exposed between waves were perfect. That was a wild scamper, but every risky escapade promised a meal of fish for all of us that night. To add to the appeal, Hamish found a place nearby where he could go skin-diving for bigger fish, with his new and ultra-cool speargun. I think he only ever got one – it was a kingfish – but he was happily occupied trying for hours. During all this, Mum lay on the beach, reading heavy stuff like Patrick White and Vladimir Nabokov, occasionally going for a lazy swim in the pool with our family dog, Dinah. I never saw Mum happier.

Nearer the house, the coast faced away from the Southern Ocean, and the water was calm and shallow. At low tide we could walk out to the weed line – about 500 metres. As the tide rose, fish and stingrays came with it, along with squid and crabs. With a torch and a net, more sweet seafood evening meals were guaranteed whenever we felt the urge. In later years, we had access to various boats, opening up the whiting grounds just offshore. King George Whiting is a South Australian speciality, currently selling for $70 and more a kilo in fish shops. Off Corny Point, we regularly caught specimens fifty centimetres or longer, which give up thick fillets of intense flavour, needing only a splash of lemon after a few minutes in a frypan or on the barbecue.

For the next ten or so years, we spent at least one family holiday a year in that house at Corny Point. We added surfing for a couple of years, until the regular shark sightings put the wind up all of us. South-west Australia is just about the capital of white pointers in the world, and one sight of a shadow near you on a surfboard in these waters is enough. But Pearl's pool, the spear fishing, the whiting, the long beach walks, and the other equally lovely beaches and swimming opportunities within a short drive, have been more than enough to keep me coming back ever since. Not nearly so often these days, partly because the farmhouse has succumbed almost completely to wind and rain. The toilet has dropped in on itself, the top of the underground tank, where Dad kept beer and wine cool, has collapsed, and last time I was there, a king brown snake, at least two metres long and appallingly lethal if it got the chance, was by the kitchen door. I took it as a sign to leave quietly and for ever.

Pearl, Jack, and Mum and Dad are all long gone, while we three boys are all over seventy now. I've helped to introduce new generations of people in my life to Corny Point. These days we rent shacks near the beach, where my children and grandchildren make their own memories. It's still a quiet place, just a bit too far from Adelaide to become a sought-after beach destination. My partner loves it as much as I do, and I'm sure we will go there again sometime soon. For me, the weight of the years since those boyish, careless adventures can trigger a few sad moments, but just one view of Pearl's pool from the clifftop still dispels all that.

The Shotgun

I was fourteen. It was early summer, so it must have been November/December 1960. I was intellectually precocious, reading everything available, and debating literature and politics with my father as often as I could. While my English and history teachers seemed to be impressed with my articulate take on weighty matters, such as what sort of president JFK would be, most of my friends made it clear I should concentrate on sport, shooting rabbits, cars and the remote possibility of sex. If there were other restless minds in my classes at a country high school, I never found them, so home and school were separate countries for me.

I had a well-established competitive relationship with my father. Since I was little, I had vied for his attention by being clever. At fourteen, I was I commenting airily on whether *Lolita* was Nabokov's best book, or if Rupert Max Stuart, an Aboriginal man sentenced to death for murder of a girl, was guilty or another victim of racism. And every time, I tried not to be crushed by his responses,; patronising me when he was sober, and loudly cutting me down when he was drunk.

Like most kids addicted to a parent's approval, I couldn't opt out; I just kept trying and kept getting hurt. If I knew something he didn't, he said it was trivia. If I beat him at billiards occasionally, it was because he was drunk, and/or my winning shots were complete flukes. If I got a good grade in school, it was because the standards were so much lower than when he studied. It makes little sense now, but I kept dreaming of showing him I was just as smart as him; a bad lesson for life, and one that took me decades to unlearn. One of his friends took me aside one day and warned me I would never beat Dad in an argument, drunk or sober. He said I should 'be my own man', but I didn't listen.

Looking back, I can see now that I was important to him. While he always made sure that he came out on top, I think he enjoyed time with me; was proud of me but had no way to show that. When my mother was close to death, she told me he had loved sparring with me about all sorts of ideas. We shared the joy of looking at all sides of an issue, sometimes having a great laugh together about some silly pronouncement in the newspapers. No topics were out of bounds – religion, politics, economics, sex – I was making sage remarks about topics about which I didn't really have a clue, and I felt like a real grown-up. Those joyous moments were the classic intermittent reinforcement that kept Pavlov's dogs coming back for more, sometimes long after any chance of getting food or praise.

Alcohol was a constant in our household. I guess there were days when Dad managed to have a good time without it, but I can't recall many now. It was a tiresome business at best, and deeply unpleasant and lonely at worst. He was never physically abusive, but every other drunken behaviour made our house a place to avoid after he had a few drinks. With Mum often in tears and my brothers keeping well out of the way, it was usually me, the faithful puppy looking for love, who became his company when a drinking mate wasn't available. My role as the family social worker was emerging, and I didn't shrink from that. Any time spent close to Dad was better than the alternatives, even if many episodes left me feeling flat and defeated. Or much worse.

One afternoon I was talking to Mum in the kitchen when Dad burst in through the back door. He was staggering drunk, red-faced, and yelling at the dogs to get out of his way. I remember wondering how he had driven home on busy roads. Mum started crying – I'm not sure why now – and he said something like, 'For God's sake don't start. You have no idea, no idea at all.' Yes, it was roughly those words – I can hear his Scottish accent now, so lovely, but for me so loaded with these memories. He banged some beer bottles down on the table, and stormed out of the room. Mum hid her head in her hands and cried harder.

I stood in the doorway, not sure how to help Mum, and worried about Dad's look of desperation. The thought that he might try to harm himself hit me, and I stepped into the hall to follow him. At that moment, a loud bang stopped me breathing. I must have been wide-eyed with fear, and I just couldn't breathe. For a few seconds, I couldn't even move. Then I hurried to his bedroom, but he wasn't there. The door to my older brother's room, where we kept two guns, was closed. Again for a moment I was frozen, couldn't go in. Then I heard him crying and swearing and thought things were OK, so I opened the door he had just terrified me by slamming.

Dad was sitting on the bed, with the shotgun open, trying to put a shell in one of the barrels. Because he was drunk and upset, he couldn't get it done. I moved over quickly, and pulled the gun out of his hands. He fell back crying, telling me life hurt too much, that I couldn't possibly know how badly, and that I should leave him alone. I took the shotgun, the shells and the .22 rifle out of the room, took them apart and hid the pieces in the linen cupboard. When I came back, he was still sobbing on the bed, and I suggested he come to his room and have a rest. He came meekly, me leading him by the hand, and lay on his own bed. I stayed for a couple of minutes, until he seemed to be going to sleep.

And that was it. I was late for swimming training, so I told Mum Dad was asleep now, and I had to go. She thanked me, and said she would be OK. Tea would be on the table at six o'clock.

I ran all the way to the swimming pool, and I am quite sure I didn't think about what had just happened. Weird, but true. I swam as the coach ordered, chatted with friends, carried on as usual. Then I ran home across the paddocks to get my tea. My brothers and Mum were just sitting down.

Mum said, 'Dad's still sleeping, so let's go ahead.'

I didn't mention anything about the shotgun, and nobody seemed to know. Actually, I'm not sure Mum ever knew; certainly, I never told her.

The next afternoon, Mum had gone somewhere with friends, and all three of us boys wanted to go out, leaving Dad at home.

I got him alone, and he said quietly, 'Don't worry, I won't shoot myself.'

We glanced at each other, and looked away. I think that was the only conversation I ever had about this with any member of my family.

So, what the hell was my psyche doing with this? I'd been beyond terror, I had coped well *in extremis*, and then said and done nothing. I think this event, and the many difficult times of minding my dad when he was drunk, did mark me in major ways, not all bad. I became an effective leader in a crisis, someone who appeared almost unnaturally calm, whatever might be happening with my pounding heart, trembling legs or tight chest. This was often useful at difficult moments, even though it could make me unable to be loving to people around me when that was most needed. That coldness was, I think, part of my misplaced conviction that I was on my own in the world. In stressful situations in later years, I believed I could not depend on support – if it happened, great; but best to assume nothing.

The incident with the shotgun can trigger reactions in me these many decades later. Something will remind me, and my emotions well up before I can clamp on a bland mask. I may feel drained and quiet for a couple days, as if it had really happened again. This sort of stuff just sits there, shaping us in subtle ways, and if we are lucky, we get some understanding and acceptance that we are OK.

Last year, with some strong encouragement, I had a discussion with my fourteen-year-old self about that day. It went like this.

'OK, you're a very frightened fourteen-year-old boy. But your dad is safe – he didn't kill himself. And your bravery is the main reason for that, so I am very proud of you. You deserve a medal, and if I could, I would hug you big time. You are just as brave as any soldier. Your dad will live for another thirty years, and became a loving father and grandpa, and it's because of you. You can go on growing up without being scared that stuff will happen again.'

It helped a lot.

Mr Hopper

Even after all this time I can't say Brian Hopper – he will always be Mr Hopper to me. Which probably means that some part of me is still that fifteen-year-old who was awed by this big, slow-moving man. Movie-star handsome, built like a brick shithouse and always immaculately dressed, he had *gravitas* to spare. He took over our Year Ten classroom for maths and science like some general with the power of life and death. His was a very quiet room, and I can't recall anyone taking him on, not even the class smart-arse, who stayed wary like the rest of us.

I guess he was not yet forty, which in those days we thought of as middle-aged. He had a stiff right arm, legacy of leaning it on the windowsill of the car when he was driving. Hit by another car, he was lucky to keep the arm, but his football career was over. South Australia may not be the centre of the sporting world, but in 1961 a guy who had been a star forward for Glenelg Football Club, before being cruelly sidelined by his injury, stood on a pretty big pedestal even before he displayed his teaching skills.

Which were very good, now I stop to think about it. With a deep, clear voice, and mastery of the blackboard, he took us through facts, theories and problems at a measured pace, always checking we were with him. Sometimes he would stand behind your desk, put his big hands on each side of your book, and softly growl something like 'Show me how this equation works. I just want to be sure you've got it. Take your time.' Over a few weeks, blind terror would gradually be replaced by the feeling you were in safe hands.

But the incident that always brings Mr Hopper to my mind is one that affected my self-esteem for many years. I should set the scene by admitting I was a very lazy boy, relying on my smarts to get me through with reasonable results without ever pushing myself. One day I'll make sense of that, given that it doesn't look anything like the adult I became, but it won't change the student that Mr Hopper found in Class 3A in Mount Barker High School. He had let me know a few times that he was unimpressed with my efforts, telling me that with my brains I should be at or near the top of the class. This day, he was checking our maths homework, set the day before.

Not unusually, after hanging out at my best friend's place, I'd had a great night listening to the radio, then read a book. Homework could wait until I got to school, when I'd race through the exercise just before maths class. By the time I realised it wasn't working out, because I hadn't been listening the day before, there he was, coming up my aisle. I started working on an excuse – I was quite gifted in that department. I polished the story as he spent time with the boy in front of me, patiently explaining his errors and helping him get it right.

Then he turned to me. As I started to speak, he made a hushing motion with his hand. After a few seconds silence, he said quietly, 'Meldrum, I just don't care.' Then walked past me to the next student.

It happened so quickly that I'm not sure if anyone else noticed. But that moment has stayed with me ever since. I felt like the least of my fellow students, a privileged, clever but spoilt and weak person who wasn't taking anything in life seriously. I was wounded, starting to concoct defences in my mind, but not believing them. And I think that part of me that pipes up in my psyche, sometimes even now, to say 'Any minute now they're going to be on to you' was shaped on that day. The hot flush when I was criticised, the angry retorts when people close to me would say I wasn't trying hard enough, were all about trying to throttle that awful feeling that flooded me when Mr Hopper told me I wasn't worth his effort.

Was that good teaching? Or just a moment of exasperation from a busy man? Was he particularly irritated by me, or barely aware of my presence? I have almost no insight into him as a person. I can't even remember if he seemed happy, although I do remember him saying something gloomy about the Cuban missile crisis, when any well-informed adult had every reason to be scared. With his star power, why was he still a classroom teacher at his age? How little I really know about someone who looms so large in my memory.

Whatever his reasons, he marked me that day. A few years ago, a colleague told me he saw signs of 'imposter syndrome' in me, which didn't make much sense to him, given my generally solid performance and achievements. 'Where do you reckon that started, David?' OK, I can weave my father and a few others into the answer, but as a simple explanation, Mr Hopper will do.

Two Caterpillars In the Desert

Going north

Going to Alice Springs was my first big adventure without my family. It was April 1964. I was just seventeen, in my first few months at university in Adelaide; a country boy who hardly knew anybody, feeling well out of my depth. My one new friend, Paul, was twenty, which seemed very mature to me. He had been working for three years at odd jobs in another area of rural South Australia, then signed on as a cadet social worker, which meant that the government was paying his fees in exchange for him agreeing to work for them for three years when he finished his degree.

Paul was a cocky, confident guy, with a strong country Australian twang. He had quite a bit of money, he'd had several girlfriends with whom he'd gone 'all the way', and he had a car. All things I wanted desperately. I tagged along around the campus, in his thrall. When Paul asked me if I was interested in joining him on a car trip to Alice Springs, I couldn't agree fast enough.

First step was to meet Paul's landlord, Peter, who, in addition to owning a couple of blocks of flats, was an earthmoving contractor. He had just finished a big job at a mine near Alice Springs, and needed his caterpillar grader and front-end loader back in Adelaide as soon as possible. Paul, with his usual chutzpah, had suggested he bring along a mate from university. The three of us could drive together to Alice Springs then bring the two heavy vehicles and the car back. We would do it for free food and drink only, in exchange for a chance to see the real outback. Peter, no doubt keen to save money, went for it, and so we met at a milk bar (no cafés in Adelaide then) to hear his plans.

Peter was about thirty-five, an olive-skinned, muscled man with an Italian-Australian accent. I thought he was a bit uncomfortable about me coming, or maybe that was just my lack of self-confidence. In any case, after a while we got on with the plan. It was going to take at least ten days: three days up, three to four coming back at slower speeds, and two to three days in Alice Springs to build two A-frames to connect the vehicles, so that we could have one big road train pulled from the front by the grader. This would save on petrol and diesel, and allow us to keep moving twenty-four hours a day, by rotating drivers.

Looking back now, it's hard to describe how excited I was. It felt like the beginning of being an adult.

I rang my mother, and airily told her I wouldn't be coming home for the university holidays, because I was going to Alice Springs to pick up a grader and front-end loader.

There was silence for a few moments.

She asked how far away Alice Springs was.

I told her: 1,600 kilometres.

More silence.

'How long will you be gone?'

When I told her, more silence.

Then she said quietly, 'Do you need any money?'

I didn't, because I had been working to pay my fees, and that was that. As I write, it hits me for the first time what that call might have felt like for her.

Two days later, Peter, Paul and I put our bags in the boot of Peter's old Holden sedan and drove out of Adelaide. I had purchased a leather travel bag, a duffel coat with 'real elk-horn' toggles, and I also brought along my brand-new, very expensive German shoes. My thinking was that I wanted to look as cool as possible when we went out on the town in Alice Springs. Duffel coat, shiny shoes, studying arts at university, what could go wrong? I was buzzing – with any luck, the days of my virginity were numbered.

In those days, the road was bitumen only until Port Augusta – the first 300 kilometres; with 1,300 more of dirt to come. The plan was to reach somewhere near Glendambo, then camp out. In April, it was still warm and mainly sunny in the daytime, so it was a pleasant enough trip, although very bumpy in the back seat after Port Augusta. But once we had set up our camp that evening, I found out a basic fact about deserts – they tend to be freezing at night. By ten o'clock it was about four degreees Centigrade and getting colder. The slight breeze cut through my fashionable but totally inadequate duffel coat. For the rest of the trip, I slept in all the clothes I had in my bag, including two pairs of socks, trying to get back to sleep when I woke up shivering, and delaying as long as I could before going out for a life-threatening pee.

After Coober Pedy, the opal mining town, the real outback began. The road became an ephemeral thing, a choice between several tracks made by previous drivers trying to avoid areas churned into impassability by road trains. Mount Willoughby, our next stop, was somewhere about 250 kilometres north of us. Peter had a compass, and if a track seemed to heading too far east, he would go left for a while, hoping to pick up the main track again. This area is criss-crossed by river beds, empty most of the time, but occasionally raging with floods that can carry large boulders and whole gum trees until the water dissipates into inland lakes which fill only every twenty years or so. Luckily, there was no rain forecast, but the deep valleys made by the rivers were often spectacularly wide, with a rocky river bed at their deepest point. If we were in the wrong place when we came to one of them, we had to work our way along until we found an established track that allowed us to go down, across and up safely.

That night was even colder, which made me very miserable later, but it was a clear black sky in the desert; my first. Paul knew all the main constellations and galaxies and so on, and kept us entertained with star-gazing stories of the Aboriginal dreamtime he had heard as a boy growing up in the country. I saw several shooting stars, and even a couple of satellites, which were rare in 1964. Paul's guide to the stars actually impressed Peter, who by now I was beginning to realise assumed that he was across everything a real man needed to know, while we were a pair of soft students who knew not much. He wasn't far wrong about me.

At Mount Willoughby we filled the tanks with petrol. The station owner told us he was amazed at how busy the road was getting. We were the tenth car through that day. 'Like Rundle Street in Adelaide out here.' He'd seen a tourist bus the day before, with about forty people on board. 'They weren't too pleased when I told them we didn't have toilets here – told them they were going to have to wait till they got to Kulgera before they could have a shit, a shower and a schnitzel.'

Kulgera is right on the South Australian/Northern Territory border, and we pulled in that evening. In the roadhouse, we were greeted by two astonishingly pretty young women behind the counter. Peter had forewarned us not to look at them for long, or try to be flirty in any way. There was no risk of that from this shrinking violet, but Paul might otherwise have tried his charming and funny best lines. Peter explained that the father, a large Greek-Australian man who was making hamburgers as we came in, was bringing the girls up on his own, his wife having left for parts unknown. His basic premise was that any man who got familiar with either of his girls would marry them or he would kill them. He kept a shotgun beneath the bar for this and related purposes. Knowing Paul quite well by now, I was very much on edge until we got out of there. A typical patter from him, such as 'Hello, darling, what's happening around here tonight – you look like you know what's going on,' and it could have all ended right there.

It was on to Alice Springs the next morning. But matters were about to get complicated. A fireside chat went very wrong that night.

Into Alice Springs

At sunrise, it was teeth-chatteringly cold in Kulgera. Two police officers passing in their patrol car stopped to chat. They had been sent from Alice Springs to catch two bank robbers who were coming north from Adelaide. This was before GPS, mobile phones and all the other ways that people can be tracked. Because all people driving north had to go through Kulgera to get fuel, all the police had to do was wait. They estimated they had about an hour to kill. What a poorly conceived escape plan. Probably the huge, isolated outback seemed like a great place to hide, but it was exactly the opposite. As duly reported in the news that night, they stepped out of the car into the waiting arms of the constables right on cue.

But that morning, Peter and I were not talking about bank robbers, or anything at all. The night before, he began to tell us about some of his sexual conquests, more bombastically with each beer. Initially it was OK, but as his contempt for women became ever more obvious, I tried to opt out of the conversation.

He got aggressive, and I should have known you can't argue with a drunk. 'What's the matter, David, you don't want to fuck women?'

I asked him how many women he had slept with, and he said it would have been about fifty. I sailed on into danger, asking him if he had considered marrying any of them.

He said no, because they were sluts, and he wanted to marry a virgin.

It was 1964, and Peter was a very conservative man, but I was still angry enough to ask him if having sex with so many women made him a slut.

Quickly he was on his feet and in my face, jabbing my chest with his finger. He was beetroot-red and he was spitting and slurring with each word. 'In this world, pal, there are the hunters and the hunted. If you don't know that, you know nothing.'

I stood my ground, legs trembling, and then he turned away, threw his beer bottle into the night and yelled over his shoulder at me to shut up and speak only when spoken to from now on.

Paul told me later that he fully expected Peter to punch me at least, if not produce the knife he often mentioned. I didn't sleep at all that night, convinced he might attack me again. The memory of that fear is so sharp: fifty-four years later, my pulse is racing as I write this.

It was a quiet, tense scene at breakfast. After speaking with the police patrol, we packed up and drove into Alice Springs.

If you haven't been there, the country is stunning. Dust as red as cayenne pepper, mountains rising purple out of the desert, huge gum trees lining creek beds, and flocks of birds, mainly brightly coloured parrots, wheeling around in a perfectly blue desert sky. The route into Alice itself is via a gorge – it feels as if you are entering another world through a magic door. We went to a gully known as Todd River and set up our tents, near encampments of Aboriginal families. Peter left us, to check out the current whereabouts of his earthmoving machines, and Paul and I had a quiet morning to write letters, explore near the area, and, in my case, catch up on lost sleep.

Peter returned late in the day, and announced we were going into town to have a meal. I considered my lovely new shoes, and my earlier optimism about such opportunities, but I was still shaken after the previous night, so my old boots stayed on. The pub we went to served up a great steak and chips, and the beer was cold. A guy Peter knew joined us, and started to tell us about 'the boongs' – the local Aboriginal people. I don't want to repeat most of the things he said – suffice to say it was raw, corrosive, hateful racism of a type I had never experienced first-hand. This was before 1967, and the referendum that gave Aboriginal people Australian citizenship, at a time when the practice known in Alice Springs as 'nigger farming' was still widespread. This consisted of collecting the pension payments for all the Aboriginal people on your property, then giving them some food – flour, sugar, beans and so on – and having them work for the cattle station without a wage. It was said that with about fifty such pensioners on your land, you got more income than you could from the cattle.

After the events of the night before, I decided to shut up. I felt dirtied somehow, stuck in a space I hated, but not saying anything. Paul was feeling the same, and back in the tent we whispered long into the night about what to do with our feelings. Over the next few decades, both of us tried to work in ways that at least addressed

Aboriginal disadvantage and marginalisation; I think Paul to greater effect than me.

Peter was in his element for the next two days – wheeling and dealing for parts for the two vehicles, the steel for the A-frames and the welding equipment. I saw a different side of him – the completely uneducated man who was naturally brilliant at mechanical tasks, and most at peace when he was doing them. I acted as unskilled assistant, not speaking unless I had to, and we got the A-frames built and attached to the vehicles in exactly the time he had predicted. The result was awesome – a twenty-five-metre-long road train; the grader in front, the front-end loader next, and the car on the back.

By the middle of the second day in Alice, Peter and I were talking fairly freely, which was a huge relief. As long as we avoided any discussion of women or Aboriginal people, we were OK. We even had a friendly debate about religion (I know, I know, I couldn't help myself risking it) in which he said he had stopped believing in God when his mum died young. We were almost on the same page on that one.

Anyway, we got the jobs done without any obvious rancour, and the whole caravan was ready to leave. That night, we went to the pub again. I felt much better, so I decided to wear my best gear, including the new shoes. Disaster! One was missing. I looked everywhere, but it has not been seen since to my knowledge. I had one perfect, unused, fine leather German shoe. Probably a week's wages for a young man down the drain, which in today's terms means at least $500. What can you do with the other one? Certainly not look cool enough to attract the right sort of attention from the young women in Alice Springs. I left Alice Springs astride a Cat 12 grader, with one shoe and none of the sensual memories I had hoped for. I kept that shoe for a couple of years, then gave in to the obvious and put out in the rubbish.

The return trip

Outside a service station, where Peter was farewelling his business partner, a dog wandered up to me, wagging its tail. As I walked to pet it, Peter appeared and told me to leave it alone. I looked up to see a man on a motorbike with sidecar looking at me intently. I froze, the dog looked disappointed, then trotted back and jumped into the sidecar. The man was wearing an old army greatcoat, and had a long beard. As he drove off, he threw me a glare that suggested I was right to back off. Peter explained that this was a lone prospector, and the dog was his only companion in the desert. Such men could get very upset if their dog received affection from anybody else.

Driving out of the town, people looked in amazement at our enormous road train, waving and calling out, 'Where are you guys off to?'

Up in the cabin, with Peter driving, I felt pretty special, with us passing out of the entrance gorge and returning to the desert in such grand style.

Peter told Paul and me about the grader's controls, emphasising that 'The handbrake is useless – never rely on it, you have to be able to come to a smooth halt without brakes.' More on that later. He also showed us how the gearbox had no synchromesh, which meant the only way to change down when in motion was to double-declutch. Best not to try was his advice; if in doubt, we should put it in neutral and coast to a stop.

I wish I had listened.

It was about twenty-five degrees Centigrade when we left. At midday it was so hot, I had stripped to a T-shirt and shorts.

But by early evening, when Peter surprised me by saying, 'All right, David, you take over,' it was cooling rapidly.

Paul and Peter retired to the car at the back, and I drove on at a stately top speed of thirty kilometres an hour. By nine o'clock at night, I was wearing all the clothes I had. The night was freezing, and I leaned close to the exhaust pipes to get some heat. Then I heard the car horn tooting. I stopped, and Peter told me they were taking the car off the A-frame, so that they could sleep, and I could go a bit faster. Forty kilometres an hour! But not for long. I had to leave the main track because it was impassable, and then found myself lost in the dark. I stopped, and turned off the motor, to see if I could get my bearings. Of course, the lights went off as well. As I climbed off, I realised it was a pitch-black cloudy night, and I could see very little. I spotted ghostly shapes, probably small trees, and heard animal noises. I felt an enormous silence closing in on me, and without warning, I got into a state of panic – I had to get the grader going and get out of here.

After a tense minute with the starter motor groaning, I actually cheered as the diesel roared into life, the lights came on, and I got the grader moving. The relief was immense, and I started singing, 'Hit the road Jack' as loudly as I could. Soon after, I found the main track, and drove along in good cheer until Peter and Paul drew alongside in the car, around two a.m. Peter congratulated me on making good speed and not getting lost. I said nothing, happy to go back to the car and get some sleep.

Late the next day, all this satisfaction and companionship came to a sticky end, and it was all my fault. I was driving alone again, with the other two back in the car, when I came to a deep river bed. I had been timing the five-mile markers, and knew I was averaging forty with the car on the back. I was chuffed, so when I saw a valley coming up, I decided to put my foot to the floor and get down and up without having to change gear. I so nearly made it. About fifty metres to go uphill, as the whole rig slowed to a crawl, I tried to double-declutch into a lower gear. I missed it with a noisy grinding of gear teeth, so I went for the handbrake. No effect, as so rightly forecast by Peter. A moment of stillness, then we started to roll backwards. When we reached the bottom, I jumped down and ran back, to find Peter and Paul scrambling out of the car, which had jackknifed to a crazy angle, but seemed undamaged.

Peter was furious of course, but so was Paul, who had feared for his life moments before.

Peter got into the grader, said, 'Get in the car now,' and started driving.

After about an hour, during which nothing was said between Paul and me, we came to the outskirts of a town called Kingoonya.

Peter stopped, came back to the car, and said, 'Get your bag out and start walking.'

Paul asked if I had any money. I said yes, although I knew I only had about $5. I waited at the side of the road as they drove away, in abject misery. It was a long walk into town, and I was feeling quite desperate just before I got there, when a farm ute pulled up alongside, and a guy said, 'Get in, mate.' He took me to the pub with no questions, other than where I was going to.

The publican looked at me, curiously dressed in a duffel coat, with the long hair of a student, and said, 'Have you got any money?'

I told him the truth, and a couple of other drinkers said, 'Get him a beer – it's on us.'

Then the publican fed me at no cost, and suggested I take a shower. Once that was done, the business of me getting back to Adelaide became the priority, with all involved making suggestions. The best idea was the train that was due in an hour or so. While the driver was in the pub, I could board one of the empty passenger cars, and hitch a ride back to Port Augusta. With the driver duly distracted by my co-conspirators, I scampered around to the far side of the train and climbed on. I hid on the floor until the train was under way, then made myself comfortable on a seat. I was exultant for a while, but soon the adrenalin ran out, and I slept for eight hours without waking.

I woke to the sound of a whistle, and realised the train was stationary. The whistle was from a man checking around the carriages in the Port Augusta rail yards. As soon as he was past my carriage, I jumped out and walked as casually as I could across the tracks to the highway. I'd done it. I was back within hitchhiking distance of home, and I still had my $5. Two truck rides later, I was in the northern suburbs of Adelaide.

I got on a bus, which cost me about fifty cents, and slumped into a seat. It all felt a bit surreal, but it hit me right then that this was exactly what I'd hoped it would be. A real adventure, without any help from my family; one I would be talking about for years to come. It was only a tiny step on the road to growing up, a journey I think is still far from finished, but I did feel a different person to the one who set out only ten days before.

Next day, on the front page of the newspaper, there was a headline and picture, without me in it, about the '75-foot road train from Alice Springs that made it to Adelaide'. Looking at Peter and Paul, dwarfed by those muddy giant machines, made me feel very alone, but I was also proud that I made it home on my own. Writing this, I feel a surge of affection for that boy who turned into me. Impatient, naive and sometimes very foolish, but brave and resourceful when it counted. A deep sense that I could take big risks and survive was being forged. Along with a hunch that my next major fuck-up would never be too far away.

A Very Slow Degree

Academically, my first few years at university were a disaster. My non-existent study habits finally caught up with me. Without the external pressures of high school teachers watching me and talking to my parents when I tried even less than usual, I went through each university subject with a cycle of just-adequate marks for assignments followed by failure at exams. I can see now that I was also out of my depth socially: from the country, with no friends at first, and feeling the ostracism of a public school boy, in a university and at a time when old money and family connections meant many of my peers arrived there with a whole cohort of friends from their private schools. The small group I became part of were none of those things, drawn together by our efforts to cope with a sense of being outsiders.

Off-campus, I was enjoying many adventures, earning quite a bit of money at various jobs, and becoming close to the woman who became my wife a few years later. But after three years I had only passed three subjects – at this rate it would take me nine years to get an undergraduate degree. I was running out of options with the university.

My father cut off my allowance after two years, but I still earned enough with various jobs to keep a roof over my head, eat and drink well, smoke expensive cigarettes, play billiards, act in amateur theatre, take my girlfriend out and go surfing whenever I wanted to. I even had a car: an ancient Chevrolet that just kept going and going with virtually no maintenance. Outside the lecture rooms, I was living the good life; inside my confidence was rock bottom and I was getting gloomy about my future. It still puzzles me why I was doing so well at every other job I took on – praised for my work ethic even – but as a student I was so lacking in confidence and bereft of any plan to get better marks. Was this the legacy of my father's constant belittling of me? I guess I'll never know and, in any case, I've always had a fierce aversion to blaming others for my troubles.

At the end of 1966, I was ready to consider anything. Eventually I made a decision not to follow a friend of mine into the merchant marine as a trainee officer, and to go to teachers' college instead. At that time, there was a small allowance, your university fees were paid, and there was a structure not unlike high school for the education subjects. I accepted I needed that structure to have a chance to turn my life around.

At first, it was a one bitter pill after another. At twenty, I was two or three years older than most of the other students, and much more radical; we didn't have much in common. I was put on probation after only a few weeks, for being seen smoking in public, hitchhiking to the college and for wearing rubber thongs instead of proper shoes. At my disciplinary interview, I was told that it would be better if I shaved off my beard.

The college principal said, 'Most of the men I've known who had beards were troublemakers with a chip on their shoulder, and some were outright communists.'

This was 1967, and his days were numbered. By the end of that year, many of the lecturers were smoking, bearded, wearing thongs, swearing and openly debating the value of school education. Scott McKenzie's 'San Francisco' was like an anthem for a growing minority of staff and students. And the first wave of baby-boomer feminism was coming on like a tsunami, throwing into question all our comfortable assumptions.

Such as the 'private talk' the college principal had with us male students. 'You have all chosen the best possible career path. Two-thirds of the students here are female. Within five years or so, most of them will be off having babies. The demographics mean that there will be a shortage of teachers for the next ten to twenty years. Play your cards right, and you'll be the principal of your own school before you're thirty.' He retired shortly afterwards; just in time to avoid the furious backlash from the women at the college that he so richly deserved.

Ironically, though, I had been right to choose teachers' college. The rigid structure worked wonders for me, and I began to pass every subject. In the middle of the year, I got engaged to be married; that also settled me down and helped me develop some regular study habits. In fact, I don't think I ever got less than a credit grade in any subject after my engagement, something for which I will be forever grateful to my ex-wife. Acting had been a passion of mine until that time. I loved the stage, and being somebody else for a change. But as the end of year exams drew close, I turned down the juicy offer of the lead role in a Beckett play, because I knew I just couldn't do both things well. The lazy boy from high school was starting to grow up a bit.

I had some scars from those first wasted years at university that didn't fade easily. Friends from high school had degrees and the well-paid jobs that went with them, while I was still in teachers' college, boosting my small allowance with odd jobs. At one stage, I had lectures from ten a.m. until three p.m. I managed to fit two jobs around that – a very early start sweeping factory floors, and a late shift three days a week driving a taxi. Sometimes I didn't have time to shower before the morning lecture, so I would have a quick wash in the toilets then sit down and try to stay awake. I still got good marks, by working hard on the weekends and the evenings, if I wasn't in the cab. Looking back, it was quite an achievement, but at the time I saw myself as a failure who had to keep running to have some chance of catching up.

After three years at teachers' college and university I had a Bachelor of Arts, a Diploma of Teaching and the Teachers Certificate that would allow me to practise. It had taken me six years to get a three-year degree, but it was done at last. Typically, Dad got drunk the day of my graduation and didn't even turn up. Mum was stoic about it, but I could see how hurt she was. He doubled down the next day by telling me that just because I had a degree, I shouldn't even imagine that I was as smart as he was. It hurt a bit, but his grip on my self-esteem was weakening – I knew I didn't have his drinking problem, I knew I was turning into a reasonably dependable worker, and that I had good potential to succeed at higher study. I was coming around to seeing him as an unhappy man who said things that I didn't need to accept. I had enough on my plate with my own self-criticisms without letting myself be upset by him any more.

That year, 1969, ended very well for me. Marriage was a great adventure, we had a funky apartment in an old mansion and a great circle of friends. The university was encouraging me to take up a master's program, and I was offered a job as a part-time tutor in the Politics Department. About to begin my first teaching appointment at a primary school in the northern suburbs, it was all coming together. The deep dents in my confidence were beginning to ease a little. They remained a major issue for many years, though. I kept defining myself by those school friends who were three years ahead of me because of my slow start, convinced they had some elusive strengths that I couldn't understand. Objectively, my work career in those years was a great success, enjoyable, fulfilling and well paid, and I did start to believe in myself a bit more. But even in my mid-thirties, a besotted parent, and a young regional director, the nagging feeling that it could all come crashing down never quite left me.

Looking back, it was nearly all wasted worry, wasted time, wasted self-absorption. But there you go – you do the best with the psyche you've got.

Being Brave

The defining issue for me in 1967 was the Vietnam war, partly because a few months before I had turned twenty. All twenty-year-old men were in a lottery, whether they liked it or not, to see if a marble with their birth date on it came up. If it did, you were conscripted into the army for two years' service, with a high likelihood of being sent to Vietnam.

As a university student studying liberal arts, I was almost naturally against the war. Only a few brave souls in my psychology and history classes supported it openly. To get a real debate going, you needed to pit economics or engineering students against us long-hairs. Outside the university, I was in a very different zone, whether at one of my factory jobs or having dinner with my girlfriend's parents. Her dad was a World War II veteran who believed we had to stop the commies in Vietnam the same way he did with the Japanese in New Guinea in 1943. Any other view was stupid and possibly traitorous. Most of the time I shut up, but we did get into a few heated arguments that ended with both of us red-faced, sullen and unpopular with the rest of the family.

Australia went 'all the way with LBJ' immediately after the USA got involved in the war in 1965, and within three years more than 200 Australian soldiers were killed and many more wounded. On campus, we talked about it every day, and many of us took part in the first of the Vietnam Moratorium marches that went on until Australia announced its withdrawal in 1972.

As my ballot came closer, I started to read up on the causes of the current conflict, and about the experiences of conscientious objectors in recent wars. In 1967, saying no would mean two years in jail, and it sounded as if that would be a hostile environment for people branded as cowards. I was beginning to realise that it was only the truly brave ones who went down that route.

In those last few weeks, I withdrew into myself on this issue, torn about what to do if my number came up. Part of me was attracted to the adventure of travelling to Asia to test myself in challenging situations. I never wanted to kill anyone, so I romanticised about being selected for intelligence work, anticipating the plans of the enemy, and working out how to 'win the hearts and minds' of the Vietnamese people. But I couldn't even fool myself with that line, knowing that whatever part you play in a war, in the end it's about who wins lethal combat, and about the hapless civilians whose lives are lost or ruined in the process.

The night before, I sat at my study desk for a couple of hours, supposedly trying to write an essay, but completely distracted. Was I prepared to go to jail? Was I completely sure that I knew what I was talking about in opposing this war? Why should other young men risk their lives if I wasn't prepared to? Could this be the biggest experience of my life, one that I would be a fool to miss? I believed I had to have this sorted before I found out about my marble, so around midnight I made a decision. I would go quietly if I was conscripted, because I didn't want to go to jail

That moment was a shocking one for me. All my commitment to the anti-Vietnam movement seemed hollow and pretentious now; I had shied away at the first hurdle. I felt pretty sure I was making the right decision, but I didn't know what it would be like to live with the consequences. I thought I might come to see myself as a coward for not sticking to my principles. I went to bed clear about my decision, but too tense to sleep. The next morning, looking in the bathroom mirror, I saw a worried stranger, someone who had arrived at this place without any clarity about why.

I went to lunch in the university refectory, and then walked with three of my friends to the building in Currie Street where the marbles were rolled around in a glass sphere. We were all jittery and a bit loud, feeling quite powerless. I didn't talk about my decision of the night before, still too confused to say anything coherent about it.

My birth date didn't come up, but my best friend's did. We went to have a beer nearby, and he talked non-stop, rattled about how to finish his studies, finish renovating his beloved MG TC, tell his girlfriend and tell his parents. He went on to be selected for officer training (largely because he was an 'old boy' from an exclusive college) and went to Vietnam. He stayed in the army, retiring twenty years later as a major.

As for me, I felt a huge anticlimax. I'd made my decision; I had to live with what I would have done, but nobody knew about the process I'd gone through. I was lucky enough to have one good conversation about that with my father a few days later. He thought it was uncannily like his own experience in World War II, where his pacifism proved very shallow when several of his best friends went off to fight, a couple never to return. He tried to enlist but, because of his scientific work, he was deemed to be in 'essential services' that had to be maintained. He said, 'You're lucky to be out of it, so just leave it at that.'

It wasn't that simple. I think those days defined me as a middle of the road type on most issues. I found myself watching passionate people exhorting the rest of us to action, and reserving my judgement about whether they really knew what they were talking about. I became much more likely to think, 'Let's see what they actually do rather than accepting what they say.' I'm happy to watch and wait until I'm a bit clearer what it is people believe in strongly enough to back themselves. I hope that makes me sceptical but not cynical. It wasn't a bad outcome overall. Over time, I came to accept that my process around the conscription issue was OK, a productive bit of growing up. I think even now it helps explain why I go with the flow most of the time, but when I make decisions, I stick to them, even if it means being a bit lonely.

Fifteen years later, I worked occasionally with a man who decided he would say no, and when his marble did come up, he went to jail. It was said had a bad time there, with most guards and fellow prisoners treating him as a coward who had let his country down. Now, as a family social worker, he was quiet, kind and widely respected. No matter how challenging our clients might be – and some were real heartbreakers for us, lurching from one terrible decision to the next – Phil stuck with them. He showed us all the meaning of 'walking alongside', when your clients have even given up on themselves. I guess we all go on different routes to find our strengths. Phil and I went opposite ways on one decision. Was he braver than me? I thought so at the time, and maybe I still do, sometimes at least, when I'm not too impressed with myself. But you can be tested any time, and I try to hold on to the memories of when I know I did do the brave thing. Everybody's got some.

Sergeant Pepper's Lonely Hearts Club Band

Yes, it's more than fifty years old, which is sobering. It's difficult today to describe the importance of the Beatles' music in 1967. I may have missed something, but I don't think any act before or since was so dominant worldwide. This album stayed number one for twenty-seven weeks in England, and fifteen weeks in the US. I can't imagine there are too many people alive today who would not recognise at least one of the songs.

I was studying at Adelaide University and the adjacent teachers college, and hub of the campus was the Barr-Smith lawns, just outside the main library. Without computers or the internet, if you needed to read a reference, you had to come to the library to do it. The grass, the low walls and a few seats to sit on would be filled with hundreds of students, especially at lunchtimes. Here those at the top of the A-list could hold court with their faithful, while us mere mortals tried to find a friendly face to share a sandwich with. It was the ultimate people-watching spot, and I hung around there too long and too often to get the higher grades I needed.

But one day in June 1967, some guys from the theatre department came to install some huge speakers, hanging them from the trees and on the roof of the locker rooms. The news spread quickly – the newest Beatles album was out, and they were going to play it full blast. Within half an hour, the area was jam-packed, and the whiff of dope smoked by the most daring wafted over us.

When that first line, 'It was twenty years ago today', came after a classic guitar intro, the place went wild. People started dancing and yelling, some trying to sing along, others telling them to shut up and let us all hear it. The speakers were awesome, at least for 1967, and there were complaints from all the adjoining study areas that no one could hear the lecturers trying to teach. Many gave up, and streams of students kept joining from 'serious' faculties like medicine, law, engineering and even economics, the people we arty types thought incapable of aesthetic emotions.

A little over half an hour later, the last crashing chords of 'A day in the life', which many critics think of as their finest work, faded away, leaving almost total silence across the lawns. We were stunned. Great art can leave you speechless, in fact it should, while you process something overwhelmingly new and important. Conversations began quietly, and people began to drift away to usual campus life. Of course, we all went out and bought, borrowed or pirated copies of the album over the next weeks. I went to at least two parties that were specifically about listening to it, while we drank bad wine and smoked the foulest cigarettes we could stand. But nothing compared to the shock of the new shared with an awed crowd, the day *Sergeant Pepper's* was released in Australia.

Bad Taxi Fare

'I'm stopping the car now. Could you please help. Your friend is trying to strangle me.'

I was twenty-two, driving a St James taxi to pay for university. It was about midnight and I had picked up a man and a woman outside a nightclub in Hindley Street. She was alternating between singing and abusing him for making her come home early. 'Who the fuck do you think you are? You're not my father, you know. I'm drunk and I fucking love it. The party was just getting started.' Then singing 'And then I'm not, not, not responsible, Oh no, I'm not, not, not responsible, I can't answer for the things I do. So fuck you.' Brief silence, then I hear, 'And fuck you too, you bearded cunt.' Obviously meaning me.

I really should have stayed quiet – you should never argue with a drunk – but the man was silent, no help there, so I said, 'Let's make sure we all get home safely tonight.' Condescending wanker. It was a very poor choice of words in the circumstances.

'Make sure? Make sure? Who said that was your job, cunt? You're worse than he is.' Then she lunged from the back seat and tried to throttle me.

There wasn't a lot of traffic, but I was passing a bus at that moment, and she was pulling my head back so that I could hardly see in front.

I slowed down, moved over behind the bus, banging into the kerb as I came to a stop. The man didn't do anything. She was still throttling me, so I pulled her hands off by myself, with some difficulty. Then she went for me again, coming over the back of the seat to have another go.

Finally, he acted, and slapped her hard, full on across the face.

She said, 'Ow, fuck,' and slumped back into her seat, whimpering.

I asked, with a croaky and wobbly voice, where he wanted me to drop them.

'Right here, mate. She needs to walk this off. How much do I owe you?' He paid, with no tip for my troubles.

I remember thinking, 'Tight-arsed bastard.'

She slammed her door violently as she went off with him, starting to yell again. At least she hadn't thrown up. They were the worst ones.

Then I started looking for another fare.

Part Two

A Young Careerist

The Swimming Club Minutes Secretary

As a teenager, my only claim to sporting ability was with swimming. I was near-talentless at anything relying on hand-eye coordination and balance, although I did go on to be quite capable as a billiards/pool player. The Mountain Pool Swimming Club was the focus of my social life, where I was on equal physical terms with other swimmers, and about the only place where I was brave enough to talk to girls. I missed out on most of that action, but I did start to develop friendships with what had been an alien species for an adolescent boy in a family with no girls.

I still love swimming, but the bigger legacy of those days was my introduction to work on committees. My mother was the secretary of the club, and one day she couldn't go to a meeting. She asked if I could attend and take the minutes. I looked at her handwritten minutes book, and it looked pretty straightforward. After training that evening, I stayed on, and was waiting in the meeting room when the club president arrived. He was a tall, loud, abrasive man, who I found out later had a hearing problem dating back to his days as an artillery gunner in the Western Desert. This led to him barking, 'What was that?' and 'Speak up!' whenever people spoke quietly. I spoke quietly, as I do still, so our interactions were often fraught.

In his booming sergeant-major's voice he asked, 'So, young David, what are you doing here?'

I explained, and he said it might be better if one of the other adults did the job, but by then a couple of others had walked in, and one said, 'Give the boy a go. He's a loyal member of the club.'

The president agreed on condition that I read out what I had recorded after each item.

My recall has always been good, at least so far, and I love picking the essence out of whatever is being discussed, so it all went quite well, until a long wrangle began on that old chestnut, a possible change to the monthly meeting schedule. Because the president was an active and sometimes belligerent participant about this, he forgot to check in with me for about twenty minutes. No agreement could be reached, so it was to be status quo.

He turned to me and said, 'David, read us out how you summarised all that.'

I read, 'Mr S proposed a change of meeting dates from the first Monday of the month to the first Wednesday. After lengthy discussion, it was agreed to retain the current arrangements.'

The president harrumphed loudly and asked the meeting if they were happy that most of their (and his) salient arguments had been lost to history. They not only agreed with my version, but later talked to my mother, asking her to become an ordinary committee member so that I could do the minutes from now on. She was more than pleased with that outcome. My life in meetings had begun.

I was really buzzed by the whole experience. I knew I was good with words, and that I had a good memory, but now I could see this actually led to life skills that others wanted. I could sit in a meeting with a bunch of adults, see and remember what was going on, and summarise for them in ways that they found really useful. Just as long as I was careful not to be a smart-arse, because there are people like that president in many meetings, who resent the youngster with the gift of the gab.

It was an epiphany for me. I started to listen to my dad talking about his job as manager of a local factory, and director of the parent company. It turned out to be a safe zone in our conversations; one that didn't veer to competitions that I would always lose, often painfully. For whatever reason, Dad was happy to share with me every aspect of his leadership style, and the difficult decisions of the day – and showed genuine interest when I made suggestions. Management had its hooks into me, and it would never let go.

For the next few years, I was absorbed in the adventures of growing up; getting engaged and married, getting though my university studies by the narrowest of margins, and becoming a teacher. Along the way, there were many situations with friends, fellow workers in my various part-time jobs, and with student groups, where I found myself being a facilitator, chairman, spokesperson or reporter. But I don't recall thinking about becoming a manager as soon as I had the chance. Perhaps I just assumed it to be the natural order of things for a capable, well-educated young man from a well-off family. Conversely, I did rather badly in my first few years at university, and I know that put big dents in my self-confidence.

Whatever the reasons, I was completely preoccupied by teaching and postgraduate studies until I was about twenty-four. That year, 1971, I was selected to be part of a conference on the development of 'open space' teaching settings, which put several classes with their teachers into one large area. I was surprised to find that it was a small symposium, with about thirty people participating. Half were teachers, and half were principals. In the first session, the facilitator told us we were going to swap roles. The teachers, many of us very young, would role-play being a school principal, and vice versa.

The facilitator then paired us up with one other, in the opposite roles, and gave us a problem to solve about open-space teaching. I remember the first issue we were handed was about four teachers working together in one unit. One was not pulling their weight, not helping with discipline, not preparing for lessons as agreed, and so on. How should this be dealt with? After fifteen minutes or so, the pairs reported briefly, then each person worked with someone else.

By lunchtime, I had teamed with about six principals. Initially I was hesitant: the first was a man about sixty years old, a vastly experienced and widely admired professional. But he immediately accepted that I was the decision-maker, and we had a sensible discussion that I summarised from time to time.

Each pairing worked better than the last, with several of the real principals saying very nice things about how much they enjoyed problem-solving with me in the lead. I shouldn't have been surprised: there is ample literature on how readily people fall into new roles in these sorts of experiments. But I was not just doing my part; I was also loving it. My listening, reasoning and clarifying skills fitted the situation like a glove. By the end of that day, I had made up my mind; I was going to get into a position where I could give effective leadership to help teams of people make progress on things that mattered to me. I had no plan yet, but from that day I was thinking about opportunities.

1971 was a very busy year for me. I was teaching, and struggling to do that well, although I loved it. I was also studying political science, doing what was called a Masters Preliminary, the equivalent of an honours year, and tutoring first-year politics students at university two evenings a week. I was at a crossroads. If I really buckled down and applied myself more to the tutoring, I could see an academic career beckoning. It was fun, but my heart was in the leadership thing now, and I had a view that teaching at university was never going to be 'the real world', whatever that is. Late in the year, I got my chance.

I had a friend working in the 'welfare department', and he told me about an upcoming fast-track executive development scheme for outstanding candidates. The new department head had decided he needed a few people to completely disrupt the models for working with neglected children, victims of family violence, young offenders and others served by approaches that hadn't changed much since the nineteenth century. I had a preliminary interview, and everything I heard convinced me this was what I wanted. The big jump in salary wouldn't hurt, although it wasn't the main driver for me. They shortlisted me, but now I had a problem. In those days, teachers who had been assisted though college had to serve out a three year bond, and go wherever they were posted. I had been lucky with that one because of my masters' studies and because I was married with a wife who worked in Adelaide. I dodged the bullet that saw friends doing three years in one-teacher schools in remote country regions.

Leaving the Education Department a year before my bond expired was regarded as career suicide, as well as risking a demand to pay back of all my student assistance. So I asked my principal at the time if there were ever any exceptions to this policy. He was adamant – no one could evade a bond. Then he added, 'Unless the director general himself agrees that it's the right thing. And that will never happen, so just accept that you have to wait another year.'

To the principal, after forty years of loyal service, the director general was a remote, almost mythical, figure of authority. To me, brought up in a household where my father had a very senior job, the director general was just a man who was a boss. That day, I rang his office, and his assistant said she would check his diary and get back to me within a couple of days. Very soon, I had an appointment. I told the principal, and he was so shocked he excused himself and went out to prune the roses in the school garden for the rest of the day. This was his standard response to difficulties, along with constant smoking.

A few days later, I went to head office, and met with the DG and his deputy. They asked me why I wanted to take on 'welfare' work with very difficult people. I told them the truth – I wanted to be in a position to make a difference for people who needed better government services.

The DG was quiet for a time, then said, 'The point of the bond scheme is to keep good people in the public service where they are needed. It seems to me you will be doing just that, even if you are in a different department. I'm going to tell my colleague in the Department for Community Welfare that if he wants you, he can have you.'

I got the final interview for the position of assistant supervisor in training that same week, and was offered the job. Three weeks later, my teaching career was over, and I was a management trainee. At just twenty-five, I was in a department of a thousand or so staff where I was in the senior ranks, on track to become a member of the executive. Writing about it now, the situation seems outlandishly lucky, but at the time I thought only of how much fun I was going to have. I was so young I was puzzled by the awkward reactions I got from people thirty years older than me, who I had just leapfrogged with no apparent effort. I got humbler and kinder about that sort of stuff over the next few years, but midway through 1972 I was completely absorbed with possibilities that seemed endless. I was going to be a boss, and I was going to help make a better world. The swimming club minutes secretary was on his way.

The Hill

In mid-1975, I was asked to take on the job of superintendent of a boy's reformatory in Adelaide, McNally Training Centre. The previous incumbent had left after a very scary incident that that had seen him in personal danger from a group of boys who had him trapped in a room. He was lucky to get out unhurt, but it was the behaviour of the staff who deserted him in that room that convinced him it was time to go. He remains a close friend of mine, and I know that night haunted him for years.

McNally was a preoccupation of the press at that time, because of several riots and escapes, and the wider perception that young thieves and worse were getting off with a 'slap on the wrist and a bag of lollies', as one reporter put it. My appointment made it on to the front page of the daily paper, and there was pressure on me to get the place under control and out of the newspapers as quickly as possible.

Those were heady days in the Department for Community Welfare, which was responsible for young offenders. At just twenty-nine, I was in charge of a facility with 120 staff looking after about the same number of thirteen- to eighteen-year-old boys. With long hair, a beard and wearing a leather jacket, I and people like me in the new wave of young managers were a sharp contrast to the older staff. Most of them were English migrants who had been in the army during World War II and Korea, and, in their view, they had taken on the job of running a prison for young men who needed to be straightened out. One of the senior people reporting to me had been rejected by the South African prison service as unsuitable, which made sense of the stories I heard about several incidents involving his excessive force.

The half dozen or so new people, including me, were all university-educated teachers, psychologists and social workers, keen to lead changes like banning corporal punishment, preparing the boys realistically for the lives they would return to after a period inside, and providing the basic education in reading and writing that most of them lacked. The average reading age of these fifteen-year-olds was ten, with a good twenty per cent of the boys being functionally illiterate.

The previous priorities, including such highlights as marching practice, public caning for misdeeds, and making cement bricks for the staff to take home at no cost for their own use, were being phased out against fierce resistance from the older staff. Arriving at McNally, I was greeted by the would-be South African prison officer, and taken on a tour, past lines of staff and boys standing at attention.

By the end of that day, I had asked that such welcomes stop forthwith, insisted that my car and those of other senior staff would be parked wherever there was a space and not in the superintendent's area, refused an offer of as many free bricks as I wanted delivered to my house, stopped the practice of all senior staff being brought their tea and coffee, in bone china, to their office, and asked for a report on why the boys on remand were waiting an average of six weeks to have a court report prepared, which usually resulted in their release. It helped that knew I had full backing on all these changes, from the director general down to my senior team, but the tensions between the old and the new were always simmering.

The epicentre of the old ways was the Block, a maximum-security unit for the twenty or so boys judged most dangerous or recalcitrant. With five-metre walls topped with loose bricks, a huge gate opened with a huge key, and individual cells with steel doors, it was a prison in every way. All of the staff except one had been in the English army, mainly Guards regiments, or the military police. The culture gap between them and my sort of manager was enormous. They and I knew it was in the Block that my predecessor had been set up for public failure and a high risk of injury or worse. Being 'sent to the

Block' was feared by the boys, and the threat was used regularly when trouble seemed imminent.

Actually, trouble seemed imminent almost every day. Boy-on-boy fights and bashings, allegations of staff assaults on boys and vice versa, theft, vandalism, escapes and riots all happened regularly during my first few weeks there. One night I was called on my beeper to be told there were about twenty boys in a remand unit refusing to go to bed, and threatening to smash their way out if the superintendent didn't come to hear their complaints. I had been at a party, and was a bit tipsy, but I went anyway. I strode in, took one look at the situation, and told the several staff present I was going to see what the boys wanted. The door was opened, I went in, and I heard the door closed and locked behind me. I'd been set up. Just as they had expected, my naive hubris propelled me past any pause for caution, and now I was locked in a room on my own with twenty boys, several of them much bigger than me.

One said, 'Hey, look, he's shitting himself. His legs are shaking.'

Some laughed, but I sensed many were frightened too – of what would happen to them afterwards, if the more violent ones went for me.

I was very scared, but I was so pissed off with the staff outside just watching that I started walking up and down the aisle between the beds, talking about how this was no way to get on with their lives, and how they would all be home with their families soon if they just took it easy. It started to work, but one of the tough guys told them they could 'take this cunt and shut him up'.

As a few formed a circle around me, I resorted to something I had promised myself I wouldn't do. I said, 'I haven't seen anything that would get you guys transferred to the Block – yet.'

Within seconds, everyone was lying on their beds. I strolled to the door as casually as I could, and waited for an agonising few seconds as the senior staff member on duty unlocked the door and let me out. Without a word, I walked out and drove home, stirred up, a bit ashamed of myself, but relieved not to have been hurt. I didn't sleep much, and by the morning I'd decided two things. One was that no repercussions for anyone involved would do any good. And two, I would start thinking about how to get rid of the Block altogether. I'd used it the same way it always had been and, as long as it was there, we could resort to fear and force when these kids needed us to do better.

We got to work on real change. For a start, there were kids locked up who didn't need to be. Many of them were staying far too long on remand. I had a very competent and well-informed deputy, even younger than me, and she suggested we should implement a quick turnaround on court reports. We went to see the chief justice, and he was completely supportive. Within a month, we were getting boys back to court within ten days. Since about eighty per cent were either bailed from court or given a community order, the population of the remand units plummeted. We also started making greater efforts to organise bail in the first place, so many boys were out the day after coming in on remand. As well as the natural justice of these new policies, we now had spare room for activities, spare staff to supervise and engage with the boys, and capacity to take staff offline for training, all achieved with no new resources.

Next, we talked with the local high school about having a basic curriculum on offer in McNally, supervised by the high school. Three teachers were found who were keen, and the school was operating within a few weeks. We gave the boys the option of attending school or going to the mechanical, leather and woodwork shops as always, and we were all delighted when classes filled quickly. Illiterate boys, who couldn't even read the captions in comics were progressing to normal reading ability for their age within three or four months in the school. The teachers inspired me. With their patience and ability to keep such damaged young men focused on the very things that they had failed at all their lives, they achieved more 'corrections', 'training' and 'rehabilitation' than the rest of us put together.

In the workshops, I put a stop to staff perks which were based on what amounted to slave labour. Staff brought in their cars, and the boys repaired, cleaned, resprayed and panel-beat them as required – all at no cost to staff and with no income for the boys. In woodwork, the boys had been making household items for the staff to take home. And of course, the brick-making had paved many a staff driveway or even built whole houses – all for free. To my surprise, this was the only set of changes I had to insist on with no support from any of my colleagues. Two of my senior staff had already had their cars reconditioned, and one had a new brick patio. Teamwork is the best way to get stuff done, but just occasionally leadership is very lonely.

We also decided to expand the senior staff weekly meeting to include several of the old guard, to make this a shared journey. The objective was twofold. One, to do our best to make sure boys who could be with their families instead of with us on remand got the right help to achieve that. Two, for those who had to do some time, make sure we had as fair, safe and productive an experience to offer as possible. The inclusive meetings made a big difference immediately. I watched, as one of the people who had stood and smirked while I was locked in that dormitory, joined in enthusiastically with planning a new sport and fitness program. These were good times. But it was during one such meeting that we got an awful reality check.

A worker burst in and blurted, 'There's been a fire in one of the time-out cells and there's a boy might be dead.'

I ran with him to where thick, black, acrid smoke was clearing, to find a fifteen-year-old boy being pulled from a cell. He was Aboriginal, and his dark skin was now covered in black soot. It was clear we were too late. This beautiful boy, a great footballer and always cheekily grinning, had got into trouble by refusing to stop talking back to staff, and been sent to do half an hour in a cell. Like others, he had matches stuck up his rectum or under his foreskin, and he had deliberately set his mattress alight. In a poorly ventilated small room, the poisonous smoke produced would have killed him in minutes.

After dealing with doctors, ambulance officers, the director general and even a reporter who got a tip-off, I spent some time with the worker who had put the boy in the cell. With 120 staff, we had just two who were Aboriginal, and he was one of them. He had taken the boy to the cell, locked him in and forgotten to go back and check after the mandatory five minutes. Usually a confident, cheerful person, he was hollowed out, breathing hard and almost incoherent. His eyes seemed blank and lifeless, as if he was in a deep dark place. I spoke quietly, asking him to sit down and get his breath, but I got nowhere. He was unreachable. The social pressures he would face for years to come would punish him every day. It was risky enough to have been paid to be one of 'the screws', but now he was forever the guy who let a 'nunga' die in a cell at McNally.

Of course, we tried to make sure it couldn't happen again. We replaced the foam mattresses, maintained constant surveillance when someone was in a cell, and, more importantly, made it a rarely used last resort, only to be used when the safety of staff or boys was at serious risk. The investigation that followed, and the later coroner's enquiry, all exposed a more authoritarian culture than even I had realised, particularly in the Block, where unrecorded use of isolation in cells had been happening every day. That tipped the balance for all of us on the senior team – it was time to find a way to close the Block. It was never going to be easy. Although the head of the staff, a stubborn defender of his regime, had just gone on extended sick leave, we knew the wider beliefs that the Block represented – discipline, 'the only thing some of these boys understand', proof that we weren't just mollycoddling hoodlums, and so on – would make it politically difficult.

Luckily for us, the architects and engineers who came to look at the safety of the cells observed in passing that the high walls of the Block were in danger of collapse within a few years at most. It took a few very heated meetings and threats of union action, and some good footwork by me with my worried bosses, but within a month we had closed the doors. Not for the last time unfortunately. After I had left, a future superintendent reopened it. I learned a lesson then – if it is there, they will use it. I applied the lesson to good effect years later when I was closing a mental hospital. Anyway, the Block walls did become unstable, so it had to be closed and demolished within another couple of years.

Gradually the ethos of the place was changing, at least on the surface. There were still perhaps twenty-five staff from the old days, and a few of them never adjusted. Although most had modest English army pensions, they were hanging out for their thirty years to get the generous South Australian superannuation, so we were stuck with each other. But now they were in the minority. With rapidly improving wages at the time, young well-educated recruits were not hard to find, with many rising to leadership roles within a year or two. About fifty per cent were women, which was a huge cultural change for the better. Attitudes about how to help young men who had been losers all their lives were becoming more positive, creative and caring. It wasn't all like that. Institutions, especially locked ones, constantly breed dysfunctional behaviours, and there were many instances of wrongdoing by staff. It's never easy to sack people, but I confess one or two opportunities to stop the rot gave me real satisfaction.

One coup was all about a kitchen door. My deputy had noticed that people often pulled up outside the back door of the kitchen when leaving work. She was sure some stealing was going on, but the head cook was adamant that could never happen with his trustworthy staff. He came to see me, accompanied by the union representative, indignant that she was ruining his good name. With no hard evidence, I had to back off, which infuriated my deputy. Only a few weeks later, a boy made a successful escape by bursting into the kitchen, threatening one of the cleaning staff with a knife, and leaving by the back door. After checking she was OK, I asked the head cook to come into work. With all the staff assembled, I told them that they would not be at risk in future, because we were going to keep the back door locked, with the key only available from the security staff at delivery times. With no exit via the back door, there would be no more escape attempts through the kitchen.

There was dead silence. Everybody was in on the racket of taking free food home from the back door. From now on, they would have to leave via the security checkpoint, bags checked like everybody else. As I reiterated that their protection was our top priority, the head cook's contorted face was a treat to watch. The food bills went down by nearly fifty per cent within a month. None of us had even guessed at the extent of the scam, which I later found out had been instituted by a previous superintendent, complete with a strict pecking order of who could take how much.

I've often reflected on how much good we did on 'The Hill', as people called McNally. For the boys we kept out of the place, by our actions around bail and quicker reporting to court, I'm sure outcomes would have been better. In any case, incarceration should always be a last resort. Some of my community-based colleagues were setting up great programs with families, finding real jobs for boys who were ready, and education and skills development for others.

For the boys who had to stay inside, I can't say I have any confidence that we turned many young lives around. I'm still sure the school was a good idea, and for some of them, I know we offered a respite from abuse, neglect and constant conditioning towards less productive and often shorter lives. And most of the new staff we recruited and trained helped to usher in a fair but firm and caring style that did less damage to already damaged boys than the old regime. I still think anyone making more than these modest claims about the benefits of youth prisons is kidding themselves.

The standout to me was how few of the boys were truly dangerous, or determined to be a criminal. Almost all of them were losers in life, used to failure, with little to look forward to. They had drifted into stealing cars, getting into fights, and falling for the triple whammy of 'abusing a police officer, resisting arrest and assaulting a police officer'. One silly bit of cheek ending with serious charges with no witnesses called except other police.

I recall only two boys I thought might be evil. One was a gang leader, and the other boys were terrified of him. Whenever some kid got his head pushed down a toilet or a knife was discovered, Tony was not too far away. He always smiled at me and said, 'Hello, Mr Meldrum. How are you?' It made me shiver. I just hoped he didn't know where I lived. It surprised no one when he got killed in a shoot-out over stolen drugs a few years later. The other nasty one raped several young women, and I was quite sure he would do it again, first chance he got. He did, and ended doing a long stretch in goal. When he was in McNally, his mother had come to see me, and screamed at me that her boy was innocent, while he smirked in the background. It's not easy to believe in reform and redemption in those moments, but thankfully they are rare.

Those boys are in their fifties now, the ones that survived. I occasionally run into or hear of some of them. A young man named William hailed me in the street one day about ten years after I left McNally. I recalled that he had asked to see me in my office on the day of his release. He presented me with a perfect copy of the master key to the whole institution. He had made it in the metalwork shop, and had been using it in secret from time to time, just for fun. He'd never told anyone about its existence, until he gave it to me. I checked it on my door – it worked. William told me he had become so interested in locks that he went on to be a locksmith, with his own successful business. He had a young family and already owned his house. Maybe he would have achieved all that and more without a spell in McNally. But I prefer to think, even if by accident, that we played a small role in helping him to hone the skills he needed to turn his life around.

Robert

The judge began to explain how today's proceedings would be conducted, but I wasn't really listening. I was troubled, not liking why I was here: to ask for an Aboriginal boy in my care to be sent to an adult jail.

Robert was seventeen and had spent most of his life in foster care or juvenile jails. With his parents both violent alcoholics, his sister already dead in a car accident, he may have felt he had little left to lose. That wasn't unusual: many of the boys in McNally were Aboriginal, and their life stories were almost uniformly depressing. But Robert was different: a leader, not because he was smarter or kinder, but because he would beat the shit out of anyone who didn't do as he asked. He ruled supreme in the Block.

It was a nasty, forbidding place, with high walls topped with loose bricks and broken glass. The boys slept in a row of cells with heavy steel doors, and the staff relished slamming them with such force that the floor shook. Most of them were ex-British army, and they saw their job as straightening these boys out, even it meant they had to break them a bit in the process. In my role as 'the Super', as they called me, I was trying to change this culture, but largely ineffectually. These men had seen off the Germans and the Japanese, and they were buggered if they were going to let a wet-behind-the-ears intellectual tell them how to do their jobs.

My agony was that it was a deputation of these very staff who had come to me requesting that I seek a court order for a boy be transferred to an adult jail. It wasn't the first time, but I had always said no in the past, because their usual position was that a boy had disobeyed too many orders, and deserved to go to jail. This was different; Robert had hurt another boy, the latest in a string of incidents. Badly this time: in a moment when staff weren't looking, he had smashed a boy's face into a toilet bowl, gashing his forehead and almost breaking his jaw. They were right on this one. I couldn't keep the other boys safe in the same space as Robert.

So a few days later, here we were in court. Only the judge, a clerk, Robert's family, their lawyer, I and a barrister supporting me were there at first, but a few police officers filed in later when I gave evidence. Robert had seriously aggravated the police time and again, especially when he filed complaints against them for assaulting him. I have no doubt his complaints were justified. I recognised a chief superintendent no less, and a couple of inspectors, all of whom had well-known dim views about people like me taking over the care of young criminals.

Robert's mother and brothers and a couple of other relatives were tightly grouped, mother crying, when the judge asked me to step up and make my case for a Section 77 order. The judge seemed to be a decent man – I thought he looked nicer than I felt about myself that day. My lawyer led me through the basics of our case, with the help of Robert's files, which showed a long history of violent behaviour.

Then it was the family lawyer's turn. He was good, and soon had me admitting that there were many incidents like this one, and that we seemed to be able to keep those offenders in McNally. I knew before he asked what his next question would be.

'Why is this situation different – why are you singling out Robert like this?'

I felt so tense and alone at that moment, the police licking their lips at the prospect of some real justice for a change, Robert himself looking at me attentively, the family angry and bereft, the lawyer fidgeting as he waited.

After a few seconds, he prompted, 'Mr Meldrum, shall I repeat the question?'

Then I knew I had to talk to Robert, to bypass all these spectators.

I felt sure I could rely on his honesty. I asked the judge, 'Your honour, in answering that question could I speak to Robert?'

The lawyer stated to harrumph, but the judge shushed him and said that sounded like a fine idea. Robert and I turned to each other.

I said, 'Robert, have you hurt other boys in McNally?'

'Yes, Mr Meldrum.'

'Have you hurt them badly?'

'A couple of times, yeah.'

'The boy this week, why did you attack him?'

'Because he had it coming.'

'Robert, think about this carefully before you answer me. If you stay in McNally, do you think you will hurt other boys?'

I guessed the lawyer would object, and he did, but the judge waved him down.

Robert didn't hesitate. 'For sure. There's lots of them deserve it.'

'You know I'm here saying the other kids aren't safe around you, so I think you have to go to Yatala jail. Can you see why I think that?'

Full eye-to-eye contact, and he straightened up and said, 'Yeah, it's probably the right thing to do.'

I looked over at the family, and again at Robert. I think we all looked worn-out at that moment, and deeply sad. But I honestly don't think any of us were angry at each other. In a fucked-up world, a very damaged and dangerous boy had just run out of options.

The lawyer said, 'No more questions, your honour.'

The police folded their arms and smiled at me. I felt angry with them. Were any of them there when some compassion and flexibility could have come up with better solutions than charges of 'abusing a police officer, resisting arrest and assaulting a police officer'. Had they beaten him personally? When would they recognise that their role in protecting community safety began with prevention, with understanding and foresight, with some love even?

The judge's quiet voice cut across this tableau. With no preambl,e he found the order to be justified, and instructed that Robert be taken to Yatala prison forthwith. I stepped down from the witness box, as did Robert. Then he crossed the floor and shook hands with me.

I said something lame like, 'Look after yourself in there.'

He said, 'Thank you,' then looked at the floor as he turned and was led away. I'm good at doing calm and composed in a crisis, but I was working hard to keep it together just then.

The chief superintendent came over to speak to me, which was something I had hoped to avoid. But he surprised me when he said, 'I guess there were no winners here today, but good on you for putting that lawyer in his place.'

In terms of mutual understanding, it was better than nothing, and I accepted the offered handshake. I bowed my head to the departing judge, and walked out with a stone in my heart.

A Very Silly Risk

In 1981, I was the district officer of the Salisbury Community Welfare Department, north of Adelaide. Somewhere in the hot January of that year, the receptionist, a tiny woman prone to grumpiness, came into my office to say that no one would respond to an urgent call from a man I'll call John, because they thought he might be dangerous.

'He's mostly bluff, but none of this lazy lot will get out there and do the job they're paid for. This man needs some help. You're the boss. In my opinion, you should either give some orders or do it yourself.'

Winning her over would have to wait. I was looking for a good distraction that day, so I went and grabbed the file, saw the address and took off in the car. Bone-dry winds were swirling leaves in the air as I parked outside a small house, with a bare front yard behind a chain-link fence. I opened the file, registering for the first time that it was very thick, to find that he was a 'serial and vexatious complainer who sometimes threatened violence when he thought he had been wronged' He had a couple of restraining orders in place, from his ex-wife and a neighbour. The Housing Trust had been trying to evict him from this house because of 'continually living in squalor', but he had refused to budge.

'What a dickhead. Should have at least read the file first,' I was thinking, not sure what to do now. There were no mobile phones then, so discussion with my colleagues wasn't an option. Then I saw the front blinds move; someone was watching me. I couldn't just sit there. As usual with me, impatient bravado prevailed and I went to the front door, my heart beating a little faster. There was a rusty screen door, and before I could knock, I heard a male voice. It was glaring sunlight outside; I couldn't see in, and when I opened the door at his request, the room looked very dark.

'If you're alone, come in slowly, and close that door behind you.'

I did and, as my eyes gradually adjusted, I saw I was in a sort of walkway between two high piles of newspapers, leading to someone sitting in a chair facing me. Medium-sized, skinny; the file said he was thirty but my impression was of an older man, although I couldn't see his face properly.

A couple of metres in front of him was another chair, and he said in a low, quiet voice, 'Just sit down there please.'

As I did so, I saw that he had a rifle in his lap, one hand near the trigger, one in front. As a teenager in the country, I had used rifles a lot, and I knew that position: ready to shoot. By now I was icy calm on the outside, heart thudding in my chest, full of regret, trying to think clearly.

I said, 'Hi, John, I'm David Meldrum, from Community Welfare. Nice to meet you.' I leant forward to shake hands and he stopped me with a hand signal. I took a chance. 'It'd be easier for me to talk if you put that gun away.'

'That's not going to happen, David.'

'OK, you called the office to ask for someone to come and see you about an urgent issue. How can I help?'

'You probably can't.'

Not the answer I wanted to hear. By now I was assessing my chances of making a run for it – zero was the obvious conclusion.

I ploughed on. 'Is this about the Housing Trust?'

'You know about that? How they think my house is filthy? Look around. What do you think?'

Well, it certainly was overfull. Every chair had a pile of books on it and the floor was covered in waist-high stacks of newspapers. With the curtains drawn and no lights on, it was hard to comment on cleanliness, but I was able to say truthfully, 'It doesn't smell dirty.'

There was a long silence. I guessed he was thinking about whether

I was being honest, or lying to keep the peace. I doubt he had a proper appreciation of how difficult it was to have a polite chat in these circumstances. But then he went on to explain why he kept the newspapers. It was sadly delusional, all about watching for patterns of reporting that showed the government's real plans for us all.

'People just aren't paying attention. The clues are all right there.'

This line of argument went on for many minutes, while I parried with such zingers as 'Do you really think so?' and 'You may have a point there.' Inane, but all I could think of that wouldn't sound patronising or even remotely combative. All the time trying not to look at the gun. I was scared to try to move the conversation to an end point, because I had a sinking feeling what that could be.

It must have been about half an hour after I came in when I took a risk and said, 'I have to get back to the office soon, John. Is there anything I can do that would be of help to you?'

Silence from him. Dry mouth for me.

Then he said, 'Tell the Housing Trust this is my house, I've been paying the rent on time for seven years, and it's not filthy like they say. I'm not moving, and if they try to evict me, I'm not going without a fight.'

I felt a crazy urge to say something honest like, 'John, this can only end badly. You just can't threaten people with guns and expect everyone to say, "Oh, all right then, you can stay."' Instead, I said, 'I can do that, John. Thanks for your time. It's been a useful meeting, and I'm quite clear what you're asking for. I'll make sure the Housing Trust understands your point of view.'

I also wanted to say, 'Can I go now, please', but I sensed that might come out in a high-pitched squeal, so I just stood up carefully and waited. He didn't move.

I said brightly, 'Well, I'll see you later.' Turned my back on him and walked very slowly between the newspaper piles back to the front door, trying to breathe evenly.

Even outside the door, the path to the front gate was directly in his line of sight; that was such a long way. It wasn't till I drove away in the car that I breathed out fully, and my hands started to shake.

He did get to keep his house. The Housing Trust people read my report and stayed away for the longest time. The mental health community team stayed away, and so did I and my team.

When I got back to the office, the receptionist was unrepentant. 'I never thought you'd just charge in there on your own. Why didn't you get the police to go with you?'

I had no good answer for that, so I shut up, and went into the lunch room, to admit to a few colleagues that I should have asked them why they were refusing to visit John. Going to the home of a man with a history of violence, on my own, with no back-up. As a community worker, I was still green behind the ears. It had been a very silly risk.

Dudley Brown

And there he was. Just as I had imagined he would look on his yacht. Over the years since the early 80s, I've sometimes wondered if I partly invented Dudley Brown. Sure, he was a colleague of mine for a couple of years, and I knew he was building a yacht, because I saw it. But the adventure he was planning, to be first to sail single-handed around the world in the twentieth century on a boat which he was building in his front yard, with no motor, seems fantastical. Especially for a man over sixty with limited sailing experience, who was a social worker in the northern suburbs of Adelaide. And yet here in 2018 was his story on a website by one of my fellow bloggers, recalling his times with Dudley in 1988 in Hawaii.

He had been in the army at the very end of World War II, training as a paratrooper. He just missed out on mortal combat, but spent time rounding up surrendering German troops. Coming to Australia after leaving the army, he went outback to work with Aboriginal Affairs departments, which at that time ran reserves that had mostly been established in the late 1800s by various Christian churches bent on conversion and moral education. With his military background, Dudley had been seen as a well-organised and resourceful man (they were always men) who could evolve into a valuable leader. By the age of thirty, he was a superintendent of a reserve – I think it was Coober Pedy in the far north of South Australia; certainly he worked there, because I remember his tales of living in a corrugated-iron house when the temperature was over fifty degrees, of course without air conditioning.

So why was he in Salisbury, a base-grade social worker, with me, twenty-five years his junior, as his boss? A bearded, weather-beaten nugget of a man, smoking constantly, who looked completely out of place in a city, let alone in a government welfare office. He claimed it was all to do with building his yacht, which was obviously impossible unless he lived near a port. And he was only a couple of years off getting his superannuation pension, and therefore wasn't too worried if the work wasn't at a level, or in an environment, that he was used to. But I did pick up snippets of another story that Dudley slid away from revealing whenever I probed gently. He had a pistol, possibly souvenired from a prisoner of war, and was happy to admit that he fired it in the air several times when drunken men on a reserve were threatening mayhem. This alone should have led to full investigations of whether his behaviour was justified. But it appeared that Dudley the cowboy superintendent was untouchable because nobody else wanted to do his job, almost alone in a bleak, isolated and very depressed township with little or no prospect of good futures for the people in his care.

I also heard a third-or-fourth-hand story that on one occasion the gun was fired at a person, resulting in serious injury, Whatever the truth of that, Dudley appeared as one of my social work staff, not wanting to talk about why, other than that his boat was slowly taking shape only a couple of kilometres down the road from our office. And that this was therefore a perfect pre-retirement posting for him. So here he was, decades older than the rest of us, and decidedly right-wing in some of his views on young offenders and child abuse, which were our chief concerns. This office was famously left-wing; in fact, I had been sent there as the district officer to bring some troublesome workers into line. Staff meetings could be a slightly surreal affair, with the rump Trotskyists refusing to do anything that our clients didn't agree with, and Dudley opining that a 'good kick up the arse' would solve many of the issues we seemed so ill-equipped to deal with. I shouldn't appear to make light of this; there were the lives of some very damaged people at stake here, and we actually made some important concessions to each other's points of view. None of us had good answers to some really awful dilemmas that we were supposed to resolve without offending anybody too much. Admitting that we were all unsure made for some grown-up thinking, and positions we found we could all work with, including Dudley.

He and I got on really well. Dudley thought I was 'officer material' who might turn out all right if I tolerated less slacking off from some of our workmates. With some mutual respect growing, the conversations turned more often to his plans for becoming a round-the-world lone sailor. I knew enough from my own sailing efforts to keep up with his stories of great deals on boat-parts, and his thinking on a design that would serve him well alone at sea. And for his crazy dream, I admired him so much. Entirely self-taught, just finishing the boat was going to be an epic achievement. I looked forward to each exposition on the best route around the world, the foods he would store, the sails he needed; even the name that he would give his boat. He wanted to call her the *Sea Eagle* because he loved those majestic birds. But the authorities said that would be easy to misunderstand on a static-filled radio call, and suggested he come up with stronger consonants.

Annoyed, he said, 'All right, call her *Podge*.'

'But why?' they asked.

'You want a word no one will mistake. *Podge* is it.' And so it was.

One day he came in to tell me had just saved himself $1,300, a large sum in 1982. He wanted the best possible wetsuit in case he fell overboard while sailing in the freezing latitudes just north of Antarctica. The salesman explained that Dudley could survive twelve or thirteen hours in the latest US Navy neoprene suit, instead of a few minutes in normal sailing clothing. Then it hit him – if he fell off his boat, it would sail on without him. There was no chance he could get back on board. So why choose a slow and miserable death? He was thinking of getting a better harness instead.

I left the Salisbury office before Dudley retired. About three year later, I met his wife Nina, who was herself now in Coober Pedy, managing the welfare office. She told me Dudley had just left Port

Adelaide on his way to Tasmania, from where he would head due south. There had been a few problems during some shakedown cruises near Adelaide, but overall the boat was behaving perfectly. He had actually done it.

I heard nothing for several years, then came a story in the media about a lone yachtsman from Australia who had gone aground in Hawaii. It was Dudley, or, as the Hawaii press had named him, 'Crocodile Dudley', because of the Australian film that had come out the year before. Local people and tourists alike had rallied to try to save his boat. The CEO of the Ford Motor Company, Lee Iacocca, had a house just above the reef where Dudley's boat was stuck, and he and Dudley became great mates for a while.

Because of the blog I found recently, I now know that his boat sank, and a 1988 version of crowd funding saw him in a new boat within a few months. He had so much charisma; the unmistakeable whiff of the authenticity of a truly free spirit. Just like me, no one could resist being part of his adventure. But it was a boat with a motor – that was one concession his benefactors insisted on. Dudley had to admit that it was the lack of an engine that saw him drift helplessly into that reef, and next time he might not be so lucky.

My fellow blogger doesn't know what happened after Dudley went around Cape Horn, via San Diego in California. If he's alive, he would be about ninety-five. I like to think he made it, or maybe he froze to death quickly in his deliberately inadequate thermal gear in the Southern Ocean. However long he lives/lived, Dudley will have done it his way, enriching the memories of all who met him.

Beating the Odds

After several unsuccessful attempts to break into the senior executive ranks of the public service, in 1982 I applied to be a regional director in the Department for Community Welfare. This one really mattered to me, mainly for a reason that seems pretty silly in retrospect. It wasn't because I could do more to shape policies to help people in need. It wasn't because I would get a pay rise. It was because I was thirty-five, and many years before I had promised myself that I would be an executive by that age. I've written before about how I was still feeling the pain of my lost years at university, a delay that had put me a few years behind the people I privately chose to compete with. Several of them had made it, but not me. With only a few months left before my self-imposed deadline, I felt a bit desperate when I was told the position would be going to someone else.

I put in an appeal against the selection decision. I knew the odds for an appeal were very long – about eight per cent were successful. I wasn't hopeful, and so I also applied for two other jobs; one as a senior lecturer in a social work faculty, and one as CEO of Adelaide's biggest non-government welfare organisation, the Adelaide Central Mission. The selection processes could not have been more different. The College of Advanced Education (soon to upgrade to be a university) interview was conducted by a panel of fourteen people. It was some sort of higher appointments committee that met infrequently, and appeared to have no structure or process. The questions seemed vague and rambling. One man slept through most of the interview. I was told they would get back to me.

The mission interview was a complete contrast. The previous CEO had been kicked upstairs to the top position in the newly formed Uniting Church in Adelaide, and he chaired the panel. Inevitably, we got around to my views on religion. There had never been anyone in their senior ranks who was not a leading member of the congregation, usually a priest. Their attention was laser-like as I answered that one. I said that if God is love, then love is God, that is, the supreme guiding principle that underpins the good and successful life of any individual or community. I also said that I had enormous respect for the radical socialist principles that Jesus taught, which gave us a very clear mission to leave no one behind in our society. I hadn't said I was a Christian, and I'm not, and I hadn't said I went to church, which I don't, but they seemed to like my answers.

Two down, one more to go. I switched my full attention back to the Appeals Tribunal, which was meeting in the same week. This was a very tense affair. Another man at my level had also appealed the decision, so he, I and the guy who had been selected were all in the tribunal, with several people from our department, who were now effectively a legal team out to squash these two appeals.

I loved this sort of situation, and I had marshalled enough of a case to show that I was 'manifestly the superior applicant' for the role. That of course involved demonstrating that neither of the other two could match my credentials. I did a reasonable job of keeping it all non-personal, but I had to prove, especially with the guy selected, that his achievements were just not adequate to take on the job of regional director. There was some very pointed repartee all round, with the tribunal members grilling us, especially on claims we made about our past employment.

That weekend, I felt a great sense of peace. I had put myself in the frame for three top jobs, any one of which I would enjoy doing, and I had come away from all three selection processes feeling I couldn't have done better. Although a win would be nice, whatever happened next was going to be much easier to accept with that knowledge.

The following Monday was extraordinary. I was notified by all three organisations that the job was mine. They all gave me twenty-four hours to think over their offer. For me, it was easy. Of course, being a CEO sounded very glamorous, and would pay the most, and working towards a doctorate while teaching social work could be a whole new way of having an exciting life. But I was very committed to public welfare services, and I wanted to play my part in making them as effective and accessible as possible. Plus, the people who I privately used as benchmarks of success were all in government executive roles. I accepted the job of regional director.

The professor I spoke to in the school of social welfare wasn't surprised. He knew me well, and he was pleased that I would be in that department at the top level. But the superintendent of the mission was furious. He said he and his colleagues had gone way out on a limb to convince the governing body of the church that this young agnostic could do a great job for them. We parted on frosty terms. And the next meeting I had was even more difficult. The director-general, my boss and now fellow member of the executive, Ian Cox, called me in to his office and closed the door. I thought he might congratulate me, let me into secrets reserved for the few, but I had misread him completely. In an angry, rambling outburst he told me I had 'destroyed a good man' who he was sure 'would have been a fine regional director'. It was going to be 'very difficult' for him to work closely with me after this 'nasty business'.

I'd never seen him like this – bitter and unforgiving – and I still don't get it completely. It was around that time he began having policy arguments with his ministerial boss in the government, which in less than two years' time would end his career. Maybe my successful appeal looked like treachery from someone he thought of as a loyal acolyte. He's long dead, so I'll never know. But a week later, we were working together, apparently happily as usual on some major issues, and it was almost as if I had dreamt those awful moments. I like to think of it as a temporary brain-fade. There was so much to admire about Ian Cox that I prefer to remember.

There I was, three weeks short of my thirty-sixth birthday, in the executive ranks at last. I had been so hungry for this, ever since my days as a primary teacher, driven by the need to put my woeful early university failures behind me; 'to join the A-team', as one colleague put it. It wasn't the end of that hunger. Wanting more doesn't just stop when you tell it to. I wouldn't feel the profound relief of finally getting that monkey off my back for another fifteen years or more. But for now, I was having some of the happiest days of my working life. Winning all the glittering prizes in one week, against the odds, is hard to beat.

16 February 1983 – *The Age* Newspaper

Emergency services were stretched beyond their limits as more than a dozen major fires around Adelaide and in the mid-north and south-east of the State took their toll in the State's worst fire in memory.

That day was always going to be very dangerous. Forty-five degrees or more in many places, and fierce gusting winds made for a freakishly high fire danger. And it turned to catastrophe, in the lushest parts of the state, the Adelaide hills, mid-north and the south-east, where the grass, bush and trees were enough fuel to make infernos.

I'd driven from Adelaide to Murray Bridge, along the south eastern freeway, and I was scanning the horizon for smoke. None so far. But the car was being buffeted by the crosswinds, and I was very pleased to have an air-conditioned car. Two hours later, seven people were to die near here, fleeing in their cars, just too late to make it out of the Adelaide hills.

I got out in Murray Bridge to find I had to lean against the wind, and I was shocked by the heat that made it hard to breathe. In the office, still not knowing if there were any fires, I decided to take a look at the State Disaster Plan. I had a vague feeling I had an official role in it. And there it was – as regional director, I was the functional services liaison officer (FSLO) for the whole south-east of the state if required. I had no idea what that meant, so I was poring over a bulky pack of materials when my deputy, Malcolm, came in to tell me there were big fires in the Adelaide hills and the south-east.

I rang the State Operations Centre, and asked what they wanted me to do.

'Get to the south-east ASAP, and start coordinating relief efforts.'

Malcolm and I jumped in a car, and set off on what would usually be a four-hour trip, which we managed in three. About an hour from Mount Gambier, the biggest town in that region, we entered the fire zone. At first, it was just smouldering bush and grasslands, but we were soon in big tree territory, and there the damage was total. Fences, sheds, vehicles and houses near the road were all smouldering ruins. Most distressingly, we saw cattle and sheep that had survived but were badly burnt, standing on the black land, surrounded by those already dead. For the next day or two, it was the job of farmers and police to shoot the survivors and organise great pits for mass graves.

In Mount Gambier, I quickly found out I wasn't needed yet. Many fires were still out of control, and while all those who died were already gone, the danger was still very real. The whole focus that afternoon and evening was on rescuing people and fighting fires. It wasn't till the next morning that I was able to tour the assembly points, where hundreds of people had slept, while rumours swirled of whole towns being consumed. I could see immediately the locals were doing very well without a state disaster plan, much as country people have always done. Food and clothing was being found, and volunteers were looking after old people and taking the children to school while their parents started to rebuild their lives. Then I got distracted by the politics of disaster. It turned out that the top brass in Adelaide had told all visiting dignitaries to contact the FSLO – me.

So the premier of South Australia, his minister of agriculture and some very senior public servants were coming. But the Governor, who has a largely ceremonial role, was also on his way, and to top that off, the prime minister of Australia was about to land at the airport. He was in the midst of a political crisis and it looked like the end of his career might be weeks away, so being seen on the front lines of disaster was too good to pass up. Accompanying this oversupply of VIPs would be a large number of reporters and cameramen. The minders of all these people were contacting me about where to start their tour. I wanted to get them all in the same place, the main assembly point, so lots of public back-patting and offers of condolence together with photographs could happen at the one time, but the prime minister's man said he wanted the PM and his wife to visit a place where there would be no one else hogging the attention.

So off we went to Tarpeena, a tiny town to the north, where half the houses were gone, and a couple of people had died. The PM, Malcolm Fraser, was a huge man, nearly two metres tall, and his wife towered over me. I arrived in time to see a phalanx of reporters lead by these two giraffe-like figures into the hall where volunteers and survivors had gathered. Mr Fraser hurried around the room, shaking a few hands, then demanded to know if the nearby fires were still burning.

So, while his wife Tammy stayed and sat with the locals, doing a great job and winning my admiration, I and all the reporters had to follow the large white government vehicle containing the PM to find the fire front. On a small dirt track, we were stopped by a fire truck, with blackened, weary men staring at all these cars and people, obviously unimpressed, as the chief explained that we could go no farther. Just then a radio call alerted them that the fire was turning back and coming our way. People started to get back in their cars, and reverse out, but the PM insisted on photographs, and strode over to lean on a fence, staring imperially towards the building smoke clouds. A few reporters got their snaps and got out as quickly as they could, but I was the FSLO, a job reserved for hardy types, so I couldn't desert my leader. Mine was the last car out, and I should confess here that it turned out to be a false alarm in any case.

Mercifully, the PM had to return to Canberra to try to save his political skin (to no avail), so it was back to Mount Gambier, where the other dignitaries were gathering at the assembly point. Again, there was no real need for me, except to spend time with all the social workers and others who worked for my department. I was going to be a glorified tour guide. The Governor approached me, and asked me to join him in his car, as it had been decided we would go to Millicent, forty kilometres to the west, to show support for victims and volunteers there. I set up the Millicent end with a couple of phone calls. When it came time to go, protocol demanded that the vice-regal car be in front of the premier's, with all others to follow. I counted fourteen cars behind us as I got into the front seat of a Rolls Royce.

The Governor was new in his job, a recently retired general, and as he shook hands and introduced his wife to me, he said, 'Isn't she a beauty?' meaning, I quickly realised, the Rolls. 'Brand-new this week. I can't tell you how fast we were going coming here, I'd get into trouble, but she goes like a rocket.'

In a Rolls, it really is so quiet you can hear the clock ticking, which is why the chauffeur had to lean in close to whisper, 'How do I get to Millicent from here?'

Now, I knew the main road, but we were in the backblocks of Mount Gambier, and I had been following other cars all day, not thinking about the route. I took a punt, and got it wrong. We did find the main road eventually, but not until a long procession of cars led by the Rolls had weaved slowly through the streets of east Mount Gambier for about fifteen minutes. Puzzled locals gazed at us, wondering, I'm sure, about our motives in inspecting these suburbs on such a day.

From Millicent, the Governor left to go back to the Adelaide hills fire sites, so I caught a ride with some bureaucrats. We took a side trip to visit a few properties that had been destroyed. We pulled up near one, where we could see a man, a woman I think was his wife, and a police officer talking, sitting on a veranda beside the smouldering remains of a house. The premier, John Bannon, asked us all to stay with the cars, forbade photos, and walked alone across the black paddock to the group. For the next fifteen minutes or so, we waited while he spoke quietly with them, arms around the man's shoulder. I never felt prouder of a politician.

As he was returning, we heard a loud noise, a sort of thunderous groaning, and we all turned to watch as a huge gum tree, most likely hundreds of years old, began to lean, then to fall. It had been burning inside for more than twenty-four hours, and had no strength left. The ground shook as the main trunk hit the ground, accompanied by many sharp explosions as the major branches snapped. We were all a bit stunned and sad; it was like watching an elephant die, finally felled by a fire that would never have been so ferocious before the nearby commercial pine forests were planted. The firestorm created was so hot that people saw flock of birds explode into flames in the air. These ancient gum trees, so majestic, were lost in large numbers that day, something nature on her own would never have allowed to happen.

Once I had seen off all these visitors, I started talking with the various groups that were at work with mopping up and welfare tasks. I could see that some people were getting fragile and frustrated by lack of coordination, so I assumed my FSLO rank and called a meeting of the heads of all agencies for that evening. It was very productive, but harrowing. I watched a young police inspector with old man's eyes describe the forensic work his team had to complete so that identifications could be certain. I felt the undercurrent of panic when the meteorologist told us the weather was hotting up again. And I heard about the apparent impossibility of getting the immediate assistance payments that the government had announced. I decided to make that my job.

The good side of this was the hugging, the offers of cooperation across agencies and the accurate information about areas of most urgent need. There was a strong feeling of pulling together that gave new energy to very tired people. I felt I'd actually kickstarted something really useful.

Next morning, I found the problem with the assistance money was that the Commonwealth government, which was covering half the cost, was insisting that every person asking for the money had to fill in a specific form together with presenting ID, forms that no one could find. I rang the operations centre, to try to get this squashed, but no dice. 'We have to minimise the chances of fraud,' I was told. The money was there, in post offices just waiting, but no one could get it. I established that the form did exist, but that because it was so rarely used, it was most likely the only stocks were in the main Adelaide post office. Five hours drive away.

Then an officer came on the phone, also a David, who I knew from a previous job. He asked me if I could authorise him to get the air force to fly the forms to Mount Gambier in an F111 fighter jet. It would only take forty minutes flying time. I airily agreed to this military deployment, and David rang me back excitedly a few minutes later to say it was all go, and he would be a passenger carrying thousands of the forms. I'm sure he was wetting himself, and it was pitiful to hear his voice when I rang back a few minutes later to tell him that a stock had just been found in Mount Gambier after all. No F111s required.

'Are you absolutely sure?'

'Yes, great idea on your part, and thanks for all your efforts. The main thing is we can start helping people now.' But I'm guessing he thought it was the worst ending ever to a boys' toy saga.

The next couple of days were full-on. I made a quick trip to Kalangadoo, a small town terribly damaged by the fires. With dead cows and sheep still lying everywhere on blackened ground, it was like some dystopian nightmare. My main purpose was to check that the financial assistance scheme was working, but I also sat down with some locals who only two days ago had been huddled together on the school oval as the fire raged around them. This included about thirty schoolchildren. I could see there were quite a few who would need to talk this out in the coming days.

Then I flew back to Adelaide in a small plane to put my case for a longer-term relief effort. There were several hundred people in deep trouble. Most of the local helpers, whether volunteering or paid, were doing wonderful work, but they were needed back in their day jobs soon. Together with a few of my local staff, led by Liz Moriarty, we had cooked up a scheme to recruit up to forty locals with the right skills and networks to work as bushfire relief workers for two or three months. Several people wanted to know how we would find that many social workers, psychologists and other health professionals who would agree to work around Mount Gambier. Liz and I agreed that was not who we were after. Watching the police, the firefighters, the teachers, the shopkeepers, insurance agents, stock and station merchants and farmers who had stepped up in the first couple of days was inspiring. These people had the skill sets we wanted, and we wanted to pay them their normal salary to be seconded to roles that many of them were already playing. My departmental boss, Ian Cox, and the premier backed the concept immediately, and I went back the next day armed with a more or less open budget.

It wasn't an easy week. My staff were tiring out, and I was a bit frazzled myself. One thing on my mind was how difficult I found it to persuade my four-year-old son that I wasn't going to be burnt in the terrible fires he saw on the news every night. While I was in Adelaide, we talked for a while, sitting in his sandpit, and I wasn't sure he believed me when I said there was no risk to me. A little boy you love staring straight into your eyes, wanting that assurance, stays with you, and I did get upset in private.

I think there were seven funerals in about three days, several for friends of my staff. But we were delighted with the enthusiasm for our scheme, and we soon had more applicants than we could handle. As we predicted, many of the people who had been in the field in the first couple of days wanted to continue helping their friends and neighbours. Our endorsement of their rightness made us many friends in the south-east.

There was so much need out there, and we had most of our new workers on the road within a week. Insurance claims, new clothes, loan cars, credit cards replaced, electricity reconnected, council rates and bank repayments deferred, fencing contractors found – the list was endless. But they were splendid. I was so impressed with these people, just getting on with it, leaning in or giving space depending on need, finding practical solutions, busting red tape in ways that never seem possible except in a disaster. It reinforced an ongoing aspect of my way of working in health and welfare settings. I didn't believe, and I still don't, that qualifications, quality standards, discipline guidelines or any of the other planks of 'professionalism' bring any guarantee that the right help in the right place will actually happen. There is often a smug certainty in that world of professionalism, and certainty has never been my companion. In that sense, even though I have social work qualifications, I wasn't really a member of any of the professional tribes.

These relief workers were helping their neighbours, so they started without detachment, but with love. They knew how to listen, and once it was clear what people wanted, they knew better than most how to make it happen. A few of them had lost their houses in bushfires past, and it was time for them to give back what their community had done for them. None of this is in the professional training handbooks for any discipline. In the years since I have been lucky enough to work with hundreds of 'para-professionals' who have come from all walks of life, especially to work in mental health services, and I remain convinced that the basic attributes of effective caring may be enhanced by more education, but are never born there. It's a view that has put me head-to-head more than a few times with health professionals, but *c'est la vie*.

As the weeks went by, I got to visit most of the townships affected by the fire, and to hear many stories, some awful, some hilarious. I'll relate just one of those.

Two men shared a house in the pine forest near Nangwarry. They were blasting contractors, so had a good supply of TNT at their place. When it was clear the fire was getting close (it was from them that I heard of flocks of parrots exploding in the sky), they decided it was too dangerous to drive with the TNT in the back of the utility. They stored it in the fridge, and got out of there. The next day they returned, not knowing what damage the fire had done.

About 400 metres from the house, on the far side of a small hill, one of them said, 'We're in deep shit.'

'Why?' says his mate.

'Because we just passed the fridge door on the side of the road.'

There was no single piece of their house left that one person couldn't easily pick up. Because the fire itself was so incredibly noisy, no one had heard what must have been a mighty explosion. I heard that the insurance company paid up. That must have been a wonderful story they concocted.

Within a couple of weeks, most of my job was done. Liz Moriarty managed the bushfire relief workers in addition to her usual role as district officer, and spoke with me often about new bits of red tape she thought I could help with.

Six weeks later, two months after the fire, we all agreed the relief workers could go back to their usual jobs. Of course, a few victims needed ongoing help, especially those who had survive great trauma and loss. That was arranged though the normal channels. But the relief workers weren't looking for a pat on the back for their bit. They didn't even want a wind-up party. They just melted back into the local woodwork, went back to their usual jobs, having achieved everything from preventing suicides to getting the phone reconnected. It was my privilege to be involved, to see how building on a community's strengths, rather than blowing into town with an 'expert' team, made so much more sense.

I went to a meeting called by the premier, to review how government services were responding to the aftermath of the fires. In the Adelaide hills and the mid-north, the largely health professional workforce was not yet fully in place, was costing nearly twice as much per worker to put in the field and administer, and were already reporting 'professional burn-out' as a significant problem. I hope I didn't sound smug when I reported from the south-east that we had completed our work, a month ahead of time, and well below the expected cost. All of us, my staff, the relief workers, the other agencies that bent over backwards to help us, and even I, the FSLO, had done a job to be proud of.

No Spilt Milk

Ian Cox, my boss from 1972 to 1984, was an extraordinary man, a visionary who could carry people with him. He was also gutsy. Before my time running McNally Training Centre, brand-new in his job, he had gone there at seven o'clock one morning, and walked in when the superintendent was caning a boy. The scene was recorded by an amateur historian as follows:

> Although not as harsh as in the old reformatory, discipline was still extremely strict. For minor infringements of the rules, boys could be placed 'on the line'. This was the removal of all privileges including smoking, weekly lolly issue, and attendance at entertainment within the Centre. A boy 'on the line' was made to run around the gymnasium for hour after hour. Those who came up to expectations received the 'privilege' of being allowed to scrub the stone floors of the ablution area.
>
> Until 1969, corporal punishment was still a feature of treatment with the Centre. After being brought back from absconding, a boy was changed into khaki shorts and shirt and placed in solitary confinement in a cabin for up to 48 hours. He was then publicly caned by the Superintendent. All the boys in the centre would form a hollow square in the gymnasium and the boy would be led into the centre of the square. The Superintendent then came into the gymnasium and the school was called to attention.
>
> Eight strokes of the cane across the buttocks were administered and the boy was then placed in a solitary confinement cabin for another 24 hours. He then received a period of up to one month 'on the line'.
>
> This was considered as a deterrent to absconding but reports of the witnessing of such public punishment indicated that it was a

sickening experience. (Dave Walsh, Weekend Notes, 11 April 2014)

Ian Cox walked straight to the superintendent and took the cane from him, saying, 'This stops now.' After regular use for a hundred years or more in this place, the cane was put away permanently.

This was only one of many sweeping changes he introduced between 1970 and 1980, including a new executive development scheme that gave me the opportunity to be part of momentous reforms. Many institutions, including orphanages, homes for girls to have their babies and then have them taken from them, rehabilitation farms in country areas and reformatories, were phased out. They were replaced with home care, intensive casework, small group homes, bail schemes, community mentors for young offenders, and 'one-stop shops' for all welfare services in the main streets of suburbs and country towns.

He did have a couple of serious blind spots, however. For one, he was rather straight-laced, and some of the new women who were moving up through the ranks of the public sector obviously rattled his sense of propriety. He would have been aghast to know how several of his executives were using drugs, especially dope, but his chauvinism made him especially likely to imagine the worst of the women amongst us. The other problem was that he was a better talker than a listener, and some very lack-lustre people got to the top because he mistook complete agreement with him for strategic intelligence. 'Yes, Mr Cox, will do, Mr Cox' could get you a long way.

In the early 1980s, the new Minister for Community Welfare became openly doubtful about Ian Cox's ability to deal with a new wave of necessary reforms, and the atmosphere at the top became increasingly tense. The minister told me one day – in the back of the ministerial car – 'I'm going to have very few opportunities to change a director general, and I'm going to make sure it happens soon.' Luckily, he made a very good choice.

Sue Vardon was only thirty-six, previously a regional director of the welfare department in New South Wales, and widely recognised as a star in the making. She had worked for the notorious Rex Jackson, who later went to jail for corruption. As her minister, he was a shocking misogynist bully, regularly yelling at his staff, throwing things at them, and using language like 'Fuck off of all you, useless cunts' when he wanted to finish a meeting. Sue said the first time this happened to her, she ran to the toilet and cried. Soon she was able to stay in control, anxious and angry, but outwardly composed. Within a couple of months of working closely with him, she was able to sit quietly while he raged, then continue where she had been cut off, as if nothing had happened.

She told me, 'Once he'd had his tantrum, I could usually get him to do what I wanted. All I had to do when he was yelling was to imagine him as a little boy naked in the bath, screaming because he didn't want his hair washed.'

By the time she got to us, her ability to stay attentive, focused and decisive under pressure was the best I have ever encountered.

I was responsible statewide for child protection and multicultural welfare services. Both had been regarded as poor career choices; child protection because there were no good answers, and multicultural matters because the head of the relevant branch was impossible to work with, but well-connected politically. As usual, I had relished taking the unpopular route, and I was delighted when Sue called me in to say I had chosen to lead in the two areas she cared about most. We spent a lot of time together, and I still look back on those days as my best education in what real leadership looks like.

I was able to take some hard, controversial decisions because I knew she would have my back, as long as I had kept her informed. Such as telling the multicultural welfare advisor that his policies were wrong in part, especially where matters of child abuse were involved. No culture believes that children should be neglected and abused, and I was not going to tell our workers to back off when a young child was being hurt because 'You don't understand what you're getting into.' We needed to do our work better in culturally appropriate ways, but his sort of advice was no help with that. After a couple of difficult meetings, which I reported to Sue, it all ended suddenly when he was charged with misuse of government resources, I think involving cars. The timing seemed too good to be true – I've often wondered if his political capital ran out just when he needed it. Anyway, now I could recruit a new, more useful, advisor.

Sue taught me so much. She wasn't just a good leader. She was the perfect package of leadership abilities. I never met anyone better at not crying over spilt milk. She could suffer a huge defeat one day, and literally have forgotten about it the next morning, as she concentrated on the next objective. For a department dominated by social workers, to have a leader who needed no time to process her feelings was very strange. It was a big bonus for me, because I'm much the same, just not as capable of a fast turnaround as she was. I asked her about it once and she said, 'The main thing is to have strong views on as few things as possible. You've got this much space to make decisions [indicating with her hands about sixty centimetres apart]. Each fixed position uses up some of that space. Choose your few with great care. Good leadership comes from the remaining free space, where you are listening with an open mind, not defending your position. I only get hurt when I lose a battle about one of my fixed ideas.'

We eventually did have a major disagreement about something that touched on one of those fixed ideas, which was that women and girls had been given a raw deal in most cultures ever since cavemen ran things. Of course, that's right. But we came to an impasse over what to do about the management of sexual abuse by the legal system. After some high-profile scandals, there was a major government inquiry into child sexual abuse. I was head of the legal responses task force. It was a volatile mixture of people: a police superintendent, a defence lawyer, a legal academic, a public prosecutor, the manager of a rape crisis centre, a doctor in charge of a sexual assault service and the director of the Children's Interest Bureau.

In our initial discussions, it was clear we agreed on very little. I only avoided total walk-outs by a hair's breadth on a few occasions, such as when the policeman referred to the rape crisis workers as 'you girls' several times in one meeting, even after I asked him not to.

Sexual abuse of children arouses the strongest possible feelings in most people, and this group was no different. The way forward ranged from 'cutting their balls off' to more therapeutic services for men, and all points between. The legal academic saved us, by suggesting we look at responses to child sexual abuse in other countries. This gave us some breathing space, as we had to wait to gather the details on several examples. In the interim, I suggested we take time to visit each other's agencies, and see for ourselves how they went about their work. I particularly remember a group of defence lawyers, who saw the whole exercise as an attack on the presumption of innocence, and the Chief Justice of the Supreme Court, who told us pompously that 'Most of these defendants are simple, brutish men of little intelligence.' When I suggested that was probably because he was only seeing the men too stupid to realise that pleading not guilty would almost certainly keep them out of court, he was frosty in the extreme. I found out later he thought I was 'a rather rude young man'.

Overall, a bit of mutual respect came out of these inter-agency jaunts, and the task force started to have productive discussions about new ways of handling legal processes. Within a few weeks, we ended up agreeing to recommend a closer look at an approach being used in Santa Clara County in California. This involved asking the alleged perpetrator not to respond to the allegations until they had watched a video, usually of their child, detailing the abuse. They were then asked to think about a maximum of ninety days in jail followed by a treatment program for two years if they chose to plead guilty immediately, or risking up to life imprisonment if they denied it and the matter went to trial. In South Australia, the rate for guilty pleas was less than five per cent (and still is). In Santa Clara, it had shot up to seventy-five per cent. We agreed to discuss this with our agency bosses.

I went to see Sue. She flat-out refused to even discuss the idea. 'I'm never going to be party to letting men who sexually assault children get off lightly.'

I ploughed on, explaining that even the rape crisis centre, a radical feminist collective, wanted to explore this, because it resulted in so many more children being believed. I repeated that the current system saw most men get off completely, while their victims were left with a lifetime among family members who didn't know who was telling the truth. Sue just repeated that there was no way she would allow further discussion. One of her fixed ideas was under attack, and she did not have the space to be a leader on this one. I glumly reported back to the working party that I couldn't get any support, to find several others had the same problem. I wasn't surprised the police had found their colleagues were unimpressed, but the defence lawyers were also outraged by this 'perversion of basic principles of the criminal law' as one Queen's Counsel put it. He actually threw my interim report across the room and stalked out.

Sue and I got on just fine on almost everything else. I found myself in a swirling rumble of discontent from many of my male colleagues, who thought ideas such as setting a target of fifty per cent of our executive group being women was a travesty. In 1987 this was fairly radical stuff, but it was way overdue. Nearly eighty per cent of our front-line workforce was female, but eight of the top twelve people in the department were male. I heard every bad joke about feminists, every male whine that we hear now from Trump et al., and I did my best to steer around it all. Things got very tense when the top three positions ended up going to women, but I look back with gratitude and admiration for all of them.

Sue went on to become the founding CEO of one of the biggest public sector organisations in Australia, Centrelink. This was after being sent to run Corrective Services by an incoming South Australian government that didn't like her style. She showed them, by reforming the prison system in two years, and becoming the 'Telstra businesswoman of the year' in the process.

I saw Sue the day she was sent to Corrective Services. It was about nine in the morning. She had already been up for hours reading about current issues in corrective services. I asked if she had any sadness about losing her previous job.

'Oh, I think I shed a few tears after the premier rang me, but that was yesterday. Do you know that our jails are sitting on ninety-nine per cent full most days? That's got to be fixed.'

Off and running; there was never going to be any spilt milk for Sue Vardon.

Part Three

So Many Adventures

A Little Piece of Mental Health Services Reform

I sat looking at the Minister of Health, and I could hear what he was saying, but it seemed so wrong; such a bad ending to a huge effort to make things work better for people affected by mental illness.

'Sorry, David, but we have no choice – we need a circuit breaker for a situation that's got out of control. You are being removed from the CEO role today. You will be suspended on full pay while we consider if there is alternate employment for you in the public sector.'

My part in the change process was closing, at least for a few years, and there was no way left for me to cling to the wreckage of a good and necessary plan.

Four years earlier, in 1988, I had moved out of my children's welfare job to become Director Mental Health Planning for South Australia. The drive towards better services in the community had stalled, and the incumbent was being asked to move on. She actually dug in – locked her office door and refused to give back the key. As so often, big bureaucracies are paralysed in the face of the unusual, and she got away with it for a week while we all waited. A year or so later, she and I were to become good friends, partly because I had come to appreciate the obstacle course on which she had stumbled and fallen.

Prima facie, the logic of reform was simple. Most patients were now ex-patients, but the hospital resources, mainly staff, had not followed them. The move out of institutional care had begun twenty years before, as the availability of new drugs combined with new policies of 'least possible restraint' began to create new options. In Adelaide, the patients had morphed mainly into psychiatric hostel residents, moving to suburbs with plentiful supplies of large old private homes that were converted into boarding houses. I came to realise that many of these were cheerless, crowded places ruled by untrained owners who treated their paying clients like unruly children. Each weekday, residents could take the special bus back to the mental hospital they came from, to attend a day program for a few hours, and see their psychiatrist as required.

As a first step in the 1960s, this had seemed like a revolution. By the time I came on the scene, more than a thousand people who had been inpatients were living out of institutional care but within this system. In 1988, almost everyone involved agreed that these people and many others with severe mental illness had a right to much better community-based options, and we knew this would involve extensive support being available to people wherever they wanted to live. The zeitgeist across the Western world was for more and better 'deinstitutionalisation', and in South Australia we were determined, as always, to claim our place as reformers delivering 'world-class mental health care'. I was to find that was a pretty vacuous phrase when it came to describing in detail what funders, practitioners, and individuals and families affected by mental illness actually wanted to happen.

I began my job, as senior bureaucrats so often do, by touring the country looking at progress across Australia. My predecessor, and the CEOs of both our mental hospitals, had done world tours, so I can at least say my junkets were modest affairs. I read widely and corresponded with leading figures in this movement internationally. My conclusion was that we were about in the middle of the reformist pack; well ahead, for example, of most states in the USA, but a long way behind some European countries and two states in Australia – New South Wales and Victoria. In at least some inner metropolitan areas of Sydney and Melbourne, resources were being moved out of mental hospitals into community support teams, and significant new funding was being added to speed up the process.

Everywhere this change was being attempted, the forces of resistance made themselves obvious. 'Mental patients on the streets' and similar headlines ratcheted up public fears, which in turn made politicians nervous. The various unions representing everybody from cleaners to doctors to social workers, nurses and administrative staff all said they were in support, so long as none of their members had to be relocated – which of course they did. In South Australia, the government, specifically the Treasury, wanted to close wards in mental hospitals to save money, not to spend it on new services if they could help it. And psychiatrists as a group were determined to control the whole game, always saying, 'Of course we all have the welfare of patients at heart', while going slow on most efforts to achieve the real change needed to deliver on that welfare.

One psychiatrist, who was also CEO of one of the mental hospitals, was proud of what he saw as 'one of the best mental hospitals in the world, and certainly a leader in Australia'. A major preoccupation seemed to be obtaining the term 'Royal' in front of the hospital's name. He had the coat of arms approved by the English College of Heralds on display in the boardroom, and said it was only a matter of a few months before this honour would be granted by Her Majesty. So, when I said that his hospital was staffed for about a thousand patients, but had no more than 200 on most days, and that this could not be allowed to continue, he saw the beginning of the end of his proudest achievements. No matter that he had to agree that 750 or more staff attending to 200 patients looked like a major misuse of public resources. Putting his hospital's 'world's best practice' at risk was not something he found easy to think about.

His solution was to propose a 'beehive' model, where most of the staff, and certainly all of the seventy or so medical staff, would continue to be based in the hospital, but buzz out to the suburbs visiting community clinics, where their patients would be waiting. All the interstate and international reformers I was talking to said it was crucial to base the staff in the communities where the people with mental illness actually lived. This was not just about being more available; it was also a necessary disruption of the narrowly medical views of mental illness that life in a medically run institution will inevitably lead to. The beehive model was likely to be more of the same with a bigger car fleet. I said that, more or less, and we locked horns from then on.

We – my little team and all the affected 'stakeholders' – stayed stuck in fruitless debate during 1989 and 1990, writing ever more detailed descriptions of a future system, while working parties, task forces, steering groups and reviews proliferated. Health bureaucracies can spend amazing amounts of time, and prodigious sums of money, while doing very little to deliver better health services to actual people. My bureaucratic bosses were reluctant to generate a brawl with the unions, especially the medicos, and I could see that the leaders of psychiatry were not too worried about the risks to their status quo. My job had seemed like a great opportunity to help achieve important change, but by now I was feeling rather impotent most days. Two years of no real progress was beginning to make me wonder if I was part of the problem.

One day I was invited by the unofficial patriarch of psychiatry in South Australia, a professor at Adelaide University, to come and 'have a good chat'. We sat in his office, and he asked me to explain what I had in mind for the future of mental health care. By then, I could do that without notes for as long as required.

He listened, apparently with rapt attention, then said, 'How interesting.' I wasn't sure what that meant, but he jumped up and said 'Come and meet a few of my colleagues.'

We walked along a corridor, and came to a door which he opened and ushered me through quickly. We were on the stage of a large lecture hall, and serried rows of doctors and nurses, perhaps a hundred of them, were waiting for their special guest, me, to speak at their 'grand round' for the week.

The professor said, 'Ladies and gentlemen, let me introduce David Meldrum, who has some interesting plans for our future. I'll leave him to explain them to you.' Then he sat in the front row, and smiled up at me innocently. He had given me no warning, and he knew it. It was a blood-freezing moment.

After what may have been five long seconds, I went for it, thanking them all for taking the time to come to listen. I talked about the basics, which I knew most of the younger doctors would at least be curious to understand, although most of them were going to leave the public system as soon as they could in any case. I stuck to a few real examples of individuals and families affected by mental illness who were doing it tough without community supports, and tried to stay away from statistics.

After about fifteen minutes, I noticed that the professor's face had turned to stone, and I knew I was making progress. The questions came thick and fast, the most insightful ones mainly from nurses. As so often, it was more about 'What's in it for me?' than 'Will this deliver better services?'

After thirty minutes, people started leaving, so I wrapped up quickly, with an invitation to talk more any time. The professor left, leaving me to find my own way out.

The next week, I was asked to come to lunch with four professors of psychiatry including my tormentor from Adelaide University.

All went well with social chit-chat until their spokesperson said, 'We have been discussing this reform process, David, and we want to offer you our full support, as long as you agree to work closely with us as your sounding board. Some of the suggestions you've made, like leadership by health professionals other than psychiatrists, just aren't going to fly, unfortunately, but in general we think you're on the right track.'

I made some vague commitments, and it ended awkwardly. But they hadn't finished yet. My informant in the professors' club told me they spoke after the lunch, and decided, 'We'll let it run for now, keep an eye on David, and if we think it has to be stopped, we will make sure that happens.' They would get me later on, but they would fail to turn back the historical tide.

This was early 1991, and a few months later the government announced a 'world class mental health plan' for South Australia. We would largely close one mental hospital, and relocate the remaining patients to the other. There were more than enough beds for this to work. About 350 staff positions would be freed up for transfer to community teams around the state. Eighty hectares of the hospital's land would be sold off for housing estates, creating the capital for more community clinics and regional hospital mental health beds. Given Adelaide's compact footprint, there were no real issues about access for families and patients, particularly since we were opening mental health wards in four general hospitals at the same time. The idea had to be kept under tight wraps until it had been thoroughly kicked around with my bureaucratic colleagues, and Treasury officials, and of course the Minister of Health. I spent time with a communications consultant who made me identify everyone who might have the ability to publicly support or criticise the plan, and it was my job to work my way through that list, talking to all of them, making sure they had a chance to be briefed in confidence just before it was made public.

The strategy was very successful, and for a short time we even had the newspapers on side. This was always going to be fragile, because it's mainly conflict and fear that excites reporters, not social justice and better use of public money. The professors struck again, getting an audience with the Minister of Health. They were discomfited to be ushered in to find me sitting beside him, but ploughed on with a denunciation of the whole process, ending with the 'shroud waving' ('Inevitably some patients will give up the struggle, Minister') that some doctors do so well. The minister promised to thoroughly review the whole plan, then bade them goodbye.

As soon as the door was closed, he turned to me and said, 'David, was that the shrill cacophony of professional self-interest, or the clarion voice of the end user?' I said I thought the former, and he said, 'I thought as much,' and asked me to press on with the plan. There was to be no review. With this guy in charge, I was in for a period of real progress.

Next, the really scary bit. Death threats, aimed specifically at me, began. For a time, I had an unmarked car, a silent phone number, and cop cars regularly cruising past our house. One incident began as a bomb threat, causing the evacuation of health headquarters. A phone caller told the terrified telephonist that the bomb would go off soon, and that it was aimed to 'get Meldrum'. An awful moment was coming out of the door on to the street, when a colleague said, 'Keep away from me, David. I don't want to get shot, it's you they're after.' Walking across Hindmarsh Square in the open made me light-headed with fear. A colleague, one the good-guy psychiatrists, asked me who the threat was to, and when I said 'It's me', his eyes widened and he stood beside me with his hand on my arm. Very brave.

I rang my wife and told her to go to her mother's place. She wouldn't take me seriously, and I had to be more forceful than I wanted, which scared her enormously. I thought the hospital staff were probably where the threats were originating, so I started going there in person, to talk with anyone who wanted more information. In the first ward I visited I was 'sent to Coventry', with all staff turning their backs on me. In another staffroom, I found a dartboard with my face on it, heavily punctured.

To break this cycle, I upped the ante, and moved in to the hospital. It was pretty ugly for a week or two, but gradually the word got around that I really did want to hear from everybody first-hand, and the oafish behaviour stopped. I often wandered the grounds, chatting with gardeners, patients, kitchen staff and health professionals, who all wanted to know what their future options would be.

At about this time, the hospital CEO came to see me in the rat-hole office they had found for me. He was agitated and hesitant at first, then blurted out, 'I think I've been wrong, David. What you're proposing makes sense, and I'm going to support you, at least till I can secure a job elsewhere.' It was clearly agony for him to do this, but I didn't take much notice of that. I thanked him profusely, and talked non-stop about what was going to happen next.

I was feeling triumphant; my nemesis had seen the light, and I was going to have a great success. He left quietly after only fifteen minutes or so, and I couldn't get on the phone quickly enough to tell my bosses that all was well. It shames me now to remember what I found out months later. At the time he came to see me, his son had recently been diagnosed with schizophrenia, and he was being driven close to his own breakdown by his son's rapid decline into unremitting psychosis that would lead to locked wards for years to come. Drained, enduring huge personal pressures, he had found the courage to have this conversation. Pride comes with a set of blinkers that stopped me from a chance to help a good man in great distress.

The two hospitals and several community clinics had been completely independent for many years. Now a new statewide organisation was formed, the South Australian Mental Health Services (SAMHS), which included hospitals and all the new community teams we were going to establish. I was much involved in that of course, so it was a bit uncomfortable applying for the CEO job that I had helped to design. Was I being impartial in proposing a new and powerful role? Mostly yes, but I did think about what a great career move this would be for me. My defence is that I didn't expect to win it, because I knew there would be keen competition from across the nation. But I did win. With invaluable help from an 'executive search' consultant, I slightly reinvented myself (beard trim, new tie and belt, new shoes and a plan to win over each member of the panel) and I aced the interview. Since my current job would no longer be needed, after only a week or so of giddy pleasure while I negotiated a salary and conditions, I became the first CEO of SAMHS. I had a great salary, a new and rather luxurious car for work and personal use, and a much-coveted Motorola Microtac mobile phone, the best boy's toy around in 1992.

And then it was down to the real work of closing a large hospital, moving about 170 patients to new accommodation, and finding new work or severance packages for hundreds of staff. For a couple of months, there was a honeymoon period, where everybody could be involved in the planning if they wanted to be. But as the first ward closure grew near, a couple of the unions began to demand delays until they secured better pay-outs for their members. The opposition in Parliament began to side with anybody who wanted the hospital left open, and they found no shortage of disgruntled staff who told them what they wanted to hear. My main concern, given that an election was not too far away, was that the opposition might dig in and say they would scrap the whole process if they got into power. And it was so easy to frighten the public with the spectre of dangerous 'mental patients' roaming the suburbs, homeless, unsupervised, and unable to control themselves. In those days, public servants like me were strongly discouraged from talking directly to the opposition, so it was difficult to build trust with them. I did break the rules and make a few useful contacts, but not to the level where favours could be called in when needed.

The biggest of many problems was the flight of doctors. At the start of 1992, there were about seventy full- and part-time medical staff, with thirty-three in the training program for psychiatrists. By June there were less than half both of those numbers, and by November, a quarter. A dozen or so medicos were not going to be relocated, as they ran the older persons inpatient and day programs for people with severe dementia. Those wards are still there, doing incredibly difficult work for few of the rewards enjoyed by other health professionals, especially psychiatrists. For the eighteen- to sixty-five-year-old inpatients, the availability of medical staff, which had previously been in almost ludicrous oversupply, had now reached the point where it was touch and go maintaining safe practice. I think we had about a dozen full-time medical staff by the end of that year. As one doctor said, it was 'tight, but doable'. The medical officers' union disagreed stridently, and found it easy to get the media interested. For me, the second half of 1992 seemed an endless round of negotiations with doctors and press interviews which almost never had a good result.

The best parts were the inputs from the fledgling consumer and carer groups, who were enthusiastic backers of the new community services. There were many bleak days when their voices were the only unmistakeably positive sign that the direction was right. I made friends there that I have today. I think that is largely because I regarded the end users as the true owners of the resources we were redirecting, and I told them so. Another bright light was those brave individuals who risked ostracism from their various professional tribes by publicly supporting the pending changes. I know one who was physically threatened; told to find work somewhere else if he valued his safety. I had to find him a job in head office, but he suffered from PTSD for some years as a result of this thuggery. Others stuck it out, joining the planning groups and workshops that gave anyone a voice if they wanted it. The 'Metropolitan and country areas mental health plan, 1993–1996' was their plan, not mine, and it outlasted me to become a reality.

Nationally, the federal government was finally playing a useful role, after decades of pretending that mental health was nothing to do with them. The First National Mental Health Plan, which I helped to write, became the first of five five-year plans so far; documents that have been the backbone of mental health policy in all states and territories since 1992. I mention this because the South Australian reform process was completely in line with the first plan, which helped me to win many an argument.

By about September 1992, I knew my days in the top job were numbered, despite being 'on time and on budget'. Industrial action was accelerating, and the sugar rush of positivity that each new service opening brought seemed to last only a few days before the next rounds of antagonism and new demands. This was no surprise – six of my interstate counterparts had been sacked or resigned under pressure in the previous twelve months. This was high-risk work. But knowing that clarified my mind and paradoxically calmed my nerves. I decided to go for broke while I could, making every day one of irreversible change for the better. When wards were emptied, and the patients rehoused in other hospitals or new residential facilities in the suburbs, I had the old buildings bulldozed immediately. I froze filling of staff vacancies in the hospital, while accelerating appointments in the new community services. And I checked in as frequently as possible with the minister and his staff, to be as sure as I could of continued backing.

That September, there was a double blow. The Minister of Health resigned suddenly, because of his wife's poor health. His replacement appeared to know nothing about mental health and, from where we sat, seemed to care even less. I couldn't even get a meeting with him, which was unnerving. In the same month, the long-serving chairman of the Health Department, my bureaucratic boss, retired. These two had been steadfast true believers and wise advisors to me for the last three years, and from then on, I was on my own in the corridors of power. With a Labour government, and every union in the health sector declaring their lack of confidence in me, each complaint to the minister became harder to deal with. Although the transfer of patients was nearly completed, and new services were opening in the community every week, I sensed that it was mainly inertia keeping the process going; inertia that would be swept aside if the political and industrial cost increased.

The leader of the opposition was having a field day. One day in November he came to the hospital and demanded to meet with all the staff. I rang my boss, but he refused to come to the phone, relaying a message via his staff for me to 'Deal with it as best you can.' I was on my own from that moment. I met with the man who the next year would become the premier of South Australia, and told him he could not come into the hospital, although I was happy to meet with him any time in his office. His offsider spoke to me quietly while we waited for the official car, referring to the long-term advantages of cooperation. I understood what he meant perfectly.

A few days later, the combined unions asked for a meeting of all staff in the hospital, except those essential to patient safety. I agreed as long as I could speak to them, and I again refused to allow the leader of the opposition to attend. He was not a legitimate player in an industrial dispute.

I was asked to stay outside until my turn to speak. I could hear people yelling and singing union songs about solidarity, as one union leader after another warmed them up. I walked on to the stage to loud booing from about five hundred staff, noticing that my legs felt wobbly and my chest tight. The cat-calling continued for a raucous minute or so, until one very loud voice in the front row called out, 'Come on, he's got guts coming in here, let's at least let him his say his piece and go.' From then on, it went well, because there were good answers to most questions raised, and the heat in the room gradually faded. I thanked them for the opportunity to speak and left a quiet room.

But it was all too late. The flashpoint came early in December, when a doctor was stabbed to death in the hospital, by a patient she had been seeing for several years. It was awful, and we were all in a state of shock. The unions, especially the doctors' association, decided this was the last straw, although her death had nothing at all to do with the closure of the hospital. I was warned by colleagues not to walk around the hospital reassuring staff, because it was somehow my fault, and feelings were running high.

A day later, my bureaucratic boss called me and suggested a retired psychiatrist, who I knew disagreed with the whole process, should become my 'co-CEO' immediately. I said no, and to no one's surprise I was called to the minister's office a couple of days later. Finally, I got to meet him, and his first and last words to me were that I, and the whole board of SAMHS, was sacked. I could go back to my office, farewell my colleagues, and leave that day. I had been in the CEO's job for eleven months. I found out the next day that the four professors of psychiatry had an audience with the minister a few hours before and persuaded him to be bold in this dark hour. It took a while, but they got me.

Because I fully expected this outcome, it didn't hurt much. I was more concerned about my planning team, who were likely to find their colleagues turning on them next. I kept in touch with several who might be at risk, and the human resources boss in head office helped to make sure they were all OK. I was sad, but proud of doing a difficult job as well as I could. I knew what I was signing on for, and I had been well paid. It was a privilege to be really useful to thousands of people affected by mental illness. The hospital closure would be completed in the next three months by my successor, who talked to me frequently, although he didn't mention this to anyone else. I knew I could rebuild a career somewhere that mattered to me, so the important thing was the chance to see a modern mental health service being born. All the conflict, time-wasting politics, report-writing, setbacks and scary moments seemed pretty insignificant compared to that. They still do.

A Few Seconds Left

13 August 1993. I guess many people would have chosen not to fly in a small plane on Friday the 13th. My wife and my secretary (yes, that was her title, it was that long ago) had both expressed concerns about the date. I remember flying into Bali, on a subsequent Friday the 13th, and the cabin erupting in cheering as the plane touched down. The conversations during the trip had been peppered with speculation about the risk we were taking, and the captain had even got into the act in ways that were meant to reassure but just fanned the flames of anxiety among the doubtful.

But in 1993 I was just excited to be going to one of the furthest Education Department schools from Adelaide, at Cook, which is near the Western Australian border, on the railway line. My job, Director of Schools, sounds much more influential than it actually was, but it got me the gig of officially opening the sports day at Cook. For reasons I can't recall, it was regarded as an important event, so four superintendents of schools came along as well. We gathered at Whyalla airport, where Graham the pilot, who was also a superintendent, was fuelling the Piper single-engine plane we were flying to Cook, via Tarcoola, and then back on the same day. From Whyalla to Tarcoola the flight was uneventful, except that we could see a front of dark clouds coming from the west. Graham told us he would reassess the weather when we were ready to leave Tarcoola.

My job in Tarcoola was to welcome the new principal and speak to the school assembly. It all went swimmingly – I confess I loved speaking at these events, being the honoured guest and so on. Back at the plane, Graham was getting a weather update on the radio, and announced that it would be OK, if a bit bumpy.

The Tarcoola principal asked for our flight plan, and I was a bit uneasy when Graham said, 'Well, do you guys want to go south first and see some whales off Ceduna?'

It seemed a bit too unplanned for flying in the outback, so I pulled rank and said we mustn't be late for the Cook sports day.

As we climbed into the plane, the principal asked again if we had a flight plan, and Graham turned to us in our seats and said, 'You quite sure you don't want to see the whales?'

There was silence – one or two of us did want to do just that, but they could see I was uncomfortable.

So Graham leaned out of the Piper and called out, 'Straight to Cook – tell them we'll be there by lunchtime.'

Within about half an hour, the cloud bank hit us. Graham first tried to get above it, but it was too big, so he went down to about 1,500 metres. It was raining heavily there, but visibility was adequate. I was reading a book and glancing at the weather occasionally, but not at all concerned – until I heard a perceptible hiccup in the engine. It stuttered for about two seconds, then ran smoothly again. I tried to get back to reading, but I noticed that Graham and his fellow superintendent and amateur pilot were huddled in conversation in the front seats. The weather was also getting worse, and I couldn't see much at all. After about ten minutes of uneventful flying, I was sitting back for a nap when the noisy drone of the engine just stopped. One cough, then nothing. The only sound was whistling wind.

For perhaps ten seconds – it may have been more or less: time wobbles in these situations – there was silence in the cabin.

Then Graham yelled loudly, 'We're fucked,' and a moment later the plane went into a near vertical dive.

I found out later that the hiccup I heard was the main tank running out of fuel, and the automatic change-over to the reserve tanks. Graham and his offsider realised immediately that we would never get as far as Cook, and were discussing where to attempt an emergency landing, when the engine died. Graham was thinking about where to glide in when he glanced at the air speed. It was decreasing rapidly, and was racing through eighty knots. He hadn't reckoned on a 100-knot headwind at this altitude. He knew that the Piper would spiral out of control and drop from the sky if it flew below seventy-seven knots. For a second, he thought it was all over, hence his panicked yell. He made a snap decision to try a deep dive to get up speed. That saved our lives.

But I knew none of that. I watched mesmerised as the Nullarbor Plain came into view, coming towards me so fast I thought I had seconds to live. There was almost no sound except the wind. My mind churned in ways that seem strange now – I was apologising to my wife and family for being so stupid, I was telling myself this was a ridiculous way to die, asking myself if it would hurt much. My thoughts hurtled through my mind so fast and so intrusively, and I can't recall if there was anyone else speaking. How long for? I'm not sure. Maybe twenty seconds.

I was so clear that this would all end in a moment, and it was a huge surprise when the plane lurched painfully out of the dive into a flat trajectory. My guess is we were no more than two hundred metres above the ground. Suddenly we were gliding quietly above scrubby desert. My mood switched to euphoric – I wasn't going to die! I was grinning, and I think I laughed out loud. Graham asked us to get braced for a rough landing, and all I could think was, 'Who cares if I get hurt, I'm going home tonight.'

When the plane hit the ground – 'touched down' doesn't do the experience justice – I became the only casualty. I was gripping the underneath of my seat so hard that the impact pulled ligaments in my elbow. It wasn't too serious, and no one else had any physical injuries. Which is amazing, because the twenty or thirty seconds we took to come to a halt were a wildly noisy, bouncing, swerving time. Small trees crashed against the wings and the undercarriage. It seemed as if the plane was completely out of control, and I fully expected it to flip over. But my relief at being alive persisted, and I remember thinking, 'What's the worst that could happen – so what if I break a leg or something? There's no fuel left so we won't go up in flames.'

The plane stopped, and there was total silence.

The first to speak was one of the superintendents, Sheila. Her words, to become legendary, were 'But I haven't brought any clean knickers.'

I followed that up with a terrible joke about some of our colleagues thinking that five less senior bureaucrats might not be all that bad. I plead temporary insanity for that one, which I hope was quickly forgotten. We stumbled out of the plane, with shaky legs, and stood in the soft rain, surrounded by ankle-deep mud.

Graham beckoned to me to come with him, and we walked back along the landing path. He said he wanted to check something that was worrying him, and he didn't want the others to get more unsettled. About three hundred metres along a branch-strewn mess, with two deep wheel ruts in the mud, we came to a spot where he said quietly, 'That was a bit close.'

A few centimetres from one rut was a rock about the size of a basketball. He saw it just after we hit, but too late to do anything, and knew it was more than enough to have caused a very nasty ending. He told me about the dive, and how close we had been to a death spiral.

I know he was heavily criticised at the later board of inquiry, but all I can say is that I'm writing this because of his quick thinking under extreme conditions. The cause was a mistake made when Graham was fuelling at Whyalla. For the first and last time in his life, he let someone else tell him when the tanks were ready. His colleague, an experienced pilot, had never fuelled a Piper, and got it wrong. The tanks were only two-thirds full. Without the bad weather, and the very strong headwinds, we might just have made it to Cook. I should add, if we had gone whale-watching, we could have run out of fuel over the Great Australian Bight, so my uncharacteristic unease about last-minute changes of plan was never so well timed.

Now we had to work out how to get out of there. We were about fifty kilometres from Cook and the only landmark visible was the railway, about a kilometre north of us. Graham got on the radio, and got no answer for several minutes. We were at the extreme range of South Australian air rescue – about 1,100 kilometres we found out later.

Eventually a crackly distant voice was found, and Graham explained our situation. As he finished, he gave our position as fifty kilometres west of Cook, and we yelled, 'No, Graham, east, we're east of Cook.'

Lucky we were listening. There was no helicopter in range, and no way to land another plane, and we were told to 'wait for the railway people to come'. We had no idea what that meant, but about an hour later a World War II-era car on train wheels appeared in the distance. We thought we would have to walk through the mud to the line, but no, it rose, came off the line, and drove across to us on large car tyres. We got in with the few things we had, on what was meant to be a day trip, went back to the railway, and the car magically switched over to train wheels.

The arrival in Cook was a bit chaotic. It had been reported that we needed urgent medical treatment, so the town ambulance was waiting. ('No need to be crook, when you're in Cook' was the sign on the door.) The sports day ceremony had been delayed while they waited to see if I was fit to play my role. And we were all being spoilt city slickers, talking about the important engagements we had in Adelaide that night – in my case, it was actually my monthly poker game, but I didn't admit that. The poker guys thought it was the best excuse I had ever come up with. 'My plane crashed' is hard to top.

It became obvious that we were going to have to stay the night. Clean knickers were obtained, beds were found, and the sports day went on; a bit late, but huge fun, even for us. Most of us were feeling powerful emotions that paradoxically made us very flat, taking over from excited relief. We all had to phone people close to us, who became instantly upset when they found out what had happened. Nothing had been on the radio or TV news – which seemed a tad unfair to us – so people were blindsided by our calls.

The board of inquiry put a stop to Graham's flying for a few months while the wheels of bureaucracy ground slowly. The Piper was stuck in the mud for weeks until a low-loader crossed the desert to take it back to Whyalla, where it needed extensive repairs. At the inquiry, it was decided that Graham would be given a last chance, which was a great relief to me.

As he was leaving the hearing, the chairman took him aside and said, 'Graham, I put this one down as FBL. Fucking bad luck.'

True, but what I remember most is the extremely good luck and skilful flying that saved my life.

Oak Valley

Sometime late in 1993 I was asked to investigate an issue that had arisen with a remote Aboriginal community in South Australia. My job was Director of Schools, which sounds very important, but with most staffing matters firmly in the grip of the human resources people, and schools funding locked in except for minor projects, I was often a guy in a suit in search of a purpose. I'm pretty sure this particular task came my way because the director general couldn't think of who else to give it to.

The story really starts in 1953, when a huge area of the outback was allocated the honour of being a test site for atomic bombs. There were several explosions in the Great Victoria Desert, regarded as so successful that a new more permanent location was needed. The Australian Supply Minister, Howard Beale, stated in 1955 that 'England has the know-how. We have the open spaces, much technical skill and a great willingness to help the Motherland. Between us we should help to build the defences of the free world, and make historic advances in harnessing the forces of nature.' So Maralinga was chosen, because it was well away from any modern towns or grazing properties. It also happened to be the home of a large community of Tjuratja Aboriginal people, who at that time had no land rights, and were not even Australian citizens. They were ordered to move out of the area to a new 'Aboriginal reserve' at a place called Yalata, near the coast that borders the Great Australian Bight.

A few people 'went bush' to avoid being forced out of their homelands, but most left on the back of trucks early in 1956. Yalata was a troubled place from the start, with the traditional leadership structures disrupted, very few local hunting grounds to obtain food, and the challenge of continual, considerable resistance from the Euro- pean community in nearby Ceduna. With jobs in very short supply, and very poor educational facilities, offending by young people, mainly men and boys, grew steadily. By 1976, when I was working in this field, a boy from Yalata had forty-four times the likelihood of being charged with a crime compared to a boy from Adelaide, where I lived.

Around 1985, more than twenty years after the last bomb testing, the leader of the Yalata community, Yami Lester, encouraged anybody who wanted to return to the traditional lands to resettle in Oak Valley, a traditional site just outside the restricted Maralinga area. This meant travelling several hundred kilometres in cars, trucks and whatever other forms of transport people could find, with no help from the government, who were against the whole idea. More than a hundred people made the journey, and set up in a valley where their people had lived for millennia. Their quality of life improved immediately. One result was that reported offences almost disappeared. With no police, no one to steal from, and the added support of the re-established Aboriginal justice system, young people were returning to hunting, making spears and other implements, weaving and building basic houses.

Within a few years, a small health centre was established, dealing with problems ranging from diabetes in epidemic proportions to skin, eye and ear diseases with young children, many the result of sleeping with dogs for warmth. Alcohol was a problem, but much less so than in Yalata, partly because now it was a very long trip to the nearest bottle shop. A very basic school was set up in the late 1980s, consisting of a couple of caravans, staffed by two non-Aboriginal teachers, usually new graduates looking for adventure.

During 1992–3, Yami Lester began pressing the Education Department for a properly equipped school in Oak Valley. The schools building people were very wary of the idea, because they knew the remote location would make for very expensive classrooms, but more than that, they couldn't be sure if the community might move again, leaving a costly white elephant sitting empty in the outback, for which someone would be blamed. But Yami was a very effective advocate, and well-known for the story of how as a boy he and his family were among those who went bush and stayed in the area when the bombs were going off. Many died, and Yami was blinded. Later, a reluctant national Australian government would cave in and pay millions of dollars in compensation, but even in 1993, a demand from Yami Lester had real clout. It was decided that the Director of Schools (me) would lead a delegation to Oak Valley to assess the feasibility of building a permanent school.

Oak Valley really is remote, even in Australian terms. It took most of two days to get to a spot roughly midway between the South Australian coast and the Northern Territory border, about nine hours travel to the nearest town. I think there were six of us, including a senior Aboriginal bureaucrat, a superintendent of schools and a high school principal. An interpreter was needed, as most of the Oak Valley people spoke only their own language (Pitjanjatjara) and a smattering of English.

When we arrived, the person designated to negotiate with us was not available, so the men were invited to go hunting for bush turkey, while the two women in our group talked with the nurse running the community health centre. I'd never been in this country before, and I was surprised by its beauty. We could see the famous red dirt of course, but long grass was everywhere, and many small trees and bushes were bright with colourful flowers. Clouds of green budgerigars swept from tree to tree, and tiny red birds (I think crimson chats) flashed around us. We men found ourselves with three well-armed locals, who drove at high speed through what looked like trackless flat country to me, then after about half an hour stopped suddenly and motioned us to keep quiet. They cocked their rifles, and were still and soundless for about five minutes. Then out of the grass came several bush turkeys. Three shots, three turkeys, and the hunting was over.

Later in the day, I wandered around the little town with the interpreter, speaking to several locals. I asked if I could see people making spears, and it happened that Jimmy (I can't recall his other name) was just beginning the crucial stage of straightening out the long thin branches. He had a cone of fine hot coals, and he moved the branches across it, twisting, bending, inspecting by eye, until he had perfectly straight two-metre shafts for the spears. Each one took about ten minutes. I got my first lesson in humility for the day when I asked if I could buy one. The interpreter spoke with Jimmy for a while, then said I would have to speak to Jimmy's agent in Adelaide, who handled all his sales.

Next morning it was down to business. The lead negotiator for the Tjuratja people was called Wayne, and he spoke only in Pitjanjatjara throughout the discussion. We sat in a circle of men in the dirt, with the women close by but off to one side, in a smaller circle.

Wayne explained their need for a school in very simple terms. 'If we want to get compensation from the government, and find new jobs for our young people, we must produce a few well-educated people every year. We will never have proper rights in this country unless that happens.'

That was fair enough in terms of community support for education, so we ticked that box. Then I asked as delicately as I could why they had chosen this particular spot to live. Which of course was code for 'Are you going to stay here if we build a school?'

Wayne talked for a long time, pausing often for the interpreter. He pointed out specific small hills, told us about a water hole that never dried up, and the 'ochre trails' that came all the way from the Northern Territory and Queensland, through Oak Valley and on to Western Australia. These were the Aboriginal equivalent of the Silk Road in Asia; trading routes for all types of goods, but especially rare ochres needed for ceremonial body-painting. He finished by saying, 'We have been exactly here for thousands of years – the only time we ever left was when you white fellas took us to Yalata.'

There was a long silence. I felt stunned and embarrassed by my ignorance, and of the colonial paternalism that we represented that day. Me, a migrant to Australia, been here for less than forty years, asking people who hadn't moved for maybe 40,000 years if they were going somewhere else any time soon. Their dignity and clarity of purpose was suddenly overwhelming.

In a perfectly timed demonstration, just at that moment there was soft excited discussion among the women. Into our group walked a teenage boy and his mother, she in bare feet. He joined the men, and explained that they had just arrived after walking from Yulara, about six hundred kilometres north of Oak Valley.

I asked through the interpreter how they survived without water for three weeks, and the boy said, 'There is water in every hole along the track, if you know the way.'

Lost Europeans have died of thirst out there regularly, but people coming to Oak Valley, barring accidents, get home in good shape every time. Never was a government building going to be more certain to be in just the right spot than the school in Oak Valley.

There was no need to summarise the meeting. They knew I had to speak to my bosses, and that government processes are never rapid or smooth. We shook hands all round, then sat down to a feast of bush turkey. It was delicious; even if I was slightly worried that we shouldn't be indulging, because only Aboriginal people are allowed to hunt this protected species. The things bureaucrats angst about.

Naturally, my report recommended that the permanent school should be built as soon as possible. I'm sorry to say that it took nine years before the following item appeared in the newspaper.

Posted 4 May 2003, 11.37a.m.

A school that was once dubbed the worst in Australia has been rebuilt and officially opened today.

The new $2 million school is at the Oak Valley Aboriginal community, on South Australia's Maralinga lands. For more than a decade, teachers described it as a Third World facility, a couple of caravans with no air conditioning in the middle of the Great Victorian Desert, where temperatures range from zero to 50 degrees. There was no running water – the only amenity, a long drop toilet.

Today, South Australian Premier Mike Rann travelled 1,000 kilometres north-west of Adelaide to officially open the $2 million school, with a childcare centre, flexible classroom spaces and new administration buildings – all air-conditioned and with amenities.

Mr Rann says it brings to an end the appalling conditions experienced by up to 60 staff and children.

I know some of the reasons for this dreadful delay that cost a generation of children a basic education. About three weeks after I returned, I lost my job, a delayed payback from a newly elected government led by a premier I had crossed swords with in a past career. That was one advocate gone. The Minister of Education lost her job as well of course, just when she had become a fierce backer for accelerating the project. In the wake of the State Bank fiasco, the new government had a lot to do, and this former priority went on to the back-burner while a swath of funding cuts were implemented.

Even now I have to accept that this situation would never have been tolerated anywhere but in a remote Aboriginal-administered township. Some hearts, including mine, were more or less in the right place, but that's never enough to defeat inequality. I think it's true that none of us are born racists, but by about the age of five most of us are developing the selective perceptions that allow us turn away from citizens who don't look or sound like most of us. The road back, to the undoing of those blind spots, seems to take more than lifetimes.

All That Jazz

Recently we went to the Helpmann Academy jazz student awards night. I've been to quite a few over the years. Actually, I helped establish the awards more than twenty years ago, when I was the first Director of the Academy. How it has grown. The prizes now total more than $15,000, compared to my first cup-rattling efforts, which raised less than $2,000. And the event has developed from when students, their families and friends and a few jazz buffs came to a hall for a performance, into a social event that the glitterati can't afford to miss. A four-course meal and wines at the Hilton, entertained by a superb eight-piece graduate student ensemble lead by an outstanding musical couple from New York, the Hot Sardines. A couple of hundred people paying $150 a head – for Adelaide, this is hitting the big time.

The skill of the graduating students lit me up as always. I love watching live music in many forms, and especially jazz. The star twenty-one- and twenty-two-year-olds can bring me to tears with their sincerity and sheer joy in playing well. I was particularly struck by the young woman on the bass, who was nailing it with flair and passion, claiming the rightful place of an instrument that so often gets lost in a band. These musicians are on the cusp of professional standards in their chosen instrument (or voice), but we all know that very few of them will break through to earning a good living from jazz. For that you need really out-of-the-ordinary skills, ridiculous amounts of luck and a single-minded drive to put music before all else. My joy at their performances is tempered with the sadness of knowing that because we can't find a way in our societies to value our best artists equally with our lawyers, scientists and business entrepreneurs, nearly all of these talented youngsters will never be professional musicians. But thank heavens they keep coming and keep striving; they will have some great adventures along the way, and our lives are enriched.

Establishing and running the Helpmann Academy for a few years was my one and only job in the arts world. When I took it on, I was advised to show no preferences, or any above-average acquaintance with any art form. Trying to bring together teachers from all the visual and performing arts meant meetings of people who had little regard for each other and suspected the worst intentions in any co-locations or joint subjects. I had to turn off my office radio, usually playing classical music, and show equal amounts of admiration for jewellery, jazz and dancing; for classical music, acting and ceramics; for painting, textiles and photography. This turned out to be no hardship, because I found joy in all of them.

The concept of the Helpmann Academy had started with a grand plan to spend large amounts of money on a new central location, named in honour of one of South Australia's most famous exports, the dancer and actor Robert Helpmann. The academy would bring together the visual and performing arts schools of the three universities in Adelaide, and the vocational education institutes (called TAFE in South Australia). In 1989, before a recession and the State Bank disaster that created a $3 billion hole in the public budget, all this had seemed feasible. With real money promised, all the players were seriously interested. We were going to take on the VCA in Melbourne, and WAAPA in Perth, and show them that the Festival City was the future of elite arts education.

Early in 1994, with a new Liberal (meaning conservative in Australia) government, the academy, which had been in the bottom of the 'pending' basket for a year or more, got a new lease of life because the premier had heard that the Helpmann family's sole survivor, Robert Helpmann's sister Sheila, might be interested in a bequest to honour Robert. But the universities and TAFE were not enthusiastic without guaranteed money on the table.

I was 'in the waiting room', the phrase used for executives who were *persona non grata* with the Liberals just then, who had been removed from their posts (Director of Schools in my case) and told to sit in their office until something was found, to be offered on a take it or leave the public service basis. I'd just been to see my old boss in the Health Department, because he wanted me to revolutionise a large institution for disabled people. I was keen but I suggested he had better check with the premier's office before we went ahead. The answer, which I could see shocked my colleague, was 'No significant jobs for Meldrum. We may have another project that he can have a go at.' I assumed this was connected with a run-in I'd had with the then leader of the opposition over the closing of a mental hospital. I'd been warned, and now it had happened.

I was told to report to the director general of TAFE for further instructions. He passed me on to his deputy, who told me my only job offer was to have a go at breathing life into the Helpmann Academy. With a young family to support, I didn't hesitate. Surprisingly, it sounded just like my sort of thing: an office, one assistant, two computers, no money and an ambitious vision nobody seemed to think would become real. An odd characteristic of my 'imposter syndrome' is that I always preferred jobs where I couldn't make things any worse. I remember a senior judge who once referred to me as a 'saviour of bad situations'. I was very happy with that reputation. What others sometimes saw as career-suicide-level bravery was actually me playing it safe.

Once I'd been confirmed as taking on the project, with the lowly title of coordinator, because the universities had made it clear nobody would be telling them what to do, I was asked to meet the premier. This was a little tense, given our history, but he got straight into explaining that my key job was to 'get the Helpmann millions for South Australia'. I hadn't realised that Robert Helpmann had come from a seriously rich family near Mount Gambier, where they ran 250,000 sheep at one time. The premier was guessing they were worth more than $100 million, and wrapped up by saying, 'That money came from South Australia, and it belongs back here.'

I had nothing to lose, so I just went for it. In the next couple of weeks, I got appointments with the three vice-chancellors and the director general of TAFE. I found them cautiously interested, but all wary of each other. It was astonishing for me to hear a couple some of these people bagging each other to someone they'd just met. I started trying to imagine how I could ease their minds, and/or leverage off that competitive energy to give the project some drive.

The best idea came from one of the VCs. 'You need a board, David, with a chairperson who has nothing to do with any of us, but is impeccably connected and powerful. That way, none of us can try to get the upper hand.'

Judith Roberts popped into my head immediately. Judith had recently achieved what was thought impossible, the closure of the Queen Victoria Maternity Hospital, to be amalgamated into an enlarged Women and Children's Hospital. She was a doyenne of old Adelaide society, known and to some extent feared as a maker and breaker of reputations. I knew she liked me, and she accepted the gig with alacrity. We met as a board not long after, with her in the chair, the three VCs and the DG of TAFE, together with several movers and shakers from the top of the corporate and philanthropic worlds in Adelaide.

On the plus side, everybody liked the idea of me chasing the Helpmann money, and in return they gave me the OK to talk with their academics about collaborative projects across institutions between complementary courses. The DG of TAFE also announced a grant of $150,000 from the government to be used to give students extra opportunities. But when one board member, the head of a major legal firm, asked if the four teaching organisations were seriously interested in benchmarking their standards against top schools inter- state and overseas, so we could work towards a claim for excellence, he got a flat no. A stony-faced, we won't be going there, flat out no. Collaboration yes, but transparent competitive standards, no way. The original concept of a world-beating centre of arts education died right there.

The collaborative projects came thick and fast. I learnt a lighter touch, giving new opportunities rather than pushing for change, such as the combined music schools' performance of the Berlioz *Requiem* at the Adelaide Entertainment Centre, which attracted 4,500 people. The Governor was there, along with heads of government departments; most of the A-list of Adelaide society came. Judith and I went to see her old family friend, the CEO of the Commonwealth Bank, who gave us $40,000 on the spot to make it happen. She had real door-opening muscle. The government minister now responsible for Helpmann had a chief of staff who was a classical music nut, and he was totally loyal to me after that night.

The two schools of acting, long contemptuous of each other, came to me to propose a merger. This gobsmacked everybody, me included. I couldn't understand the process of these warring tribes getting to this point; too many harsh words had been traded in recent years. Sadly, it lasted only a few weeks, not even making it to the first joint performance. They divorced on the grounds of irreconcilable differences and exist separately to this day. Several other projects were moving along slowly, with reasonable cooperation between like courses, but serious talk about mergers faded for a few years. Except for music, there have been none since.

I concentrated on the Helpmann money. I visited Sheila Helpmann in her amazing Elizabeth Bay apartment, one of the best bits of real estate on Sydney harbour. We hit it off immediately. I loved her endless stories of Hollywood and London, and the gossip about the rich and famous. At seventy-eight, she had seen all the golden years of Hollywood, and she knew them all. One day, Katherine Hepburn called her on the phone, and I had to wait for nearly half an hour. She liked what I had to say about the potential of the Helpmann Academy, and decided to come to Adelaide to talk to the premier and her old friend the Governor, Dame Roma Mitchell. Old friends. Old family friends. So this was how it worked.

It was a huge success. The premier was super-polite and deferential to Sheila, and she and Dame Roma spent many happy hours together. They went to the ballet one night, as the honoured guests of course.

After another trip by me to Sydney, to talk more about the future, she called me. 'David, I have decided to endow the Helpmann Academy. I had been planning to place the bulk of the money with NIDA, the Sydney Conservatorium and the Australian Ballet, but I'm rethinking all that. Robert would have wanted me to do this. When can you come over again? I'd like to take you out to a celebratory dinner.'

We agreed on two days hence. It was also her birthday that week. I sent a huge bunch of flowers which she rang to thank me for. Then, that same day, she had a massive stroke. She never regained consciousness, and died two days later. Her 'constant companion', also called Robert, called just after she died, and said he had never seen her happier than in the days before it happened. She'd loved the times she had spent with me. He added that he thought the excitement might have been too much for her, which made me feel a bit queasy. At the funeral, several people came over to congratulate me quietly, telling me they were so happy she lived long enough to endow the Helpmann Academy. But I was starting to find out that they were wrong. In Australia at that time, the fact that she had a very clear will, and had not changed it, or even given her lawyers notice that she intended to, meant we had no prospect of a bequest.

The premier was furious. I was amazed I had come that close to such a huge coup, and looking for some sign of shared sadness at the loss of a lovely lady, but he was completely focused on the money. The Crown Solicitor was called in, to give the same advice I had. After a few days of reviewing legal opinions, it was over. Those Sydney institutions, already the richest in the country, got the lot. And the Helpmann Academy's time on the shortlist of projects that might have cast a rosy glow on the new government were over.

After that, my fund-raising efforts were continual, but always at the usual Adelaide arts philanthropy level of a couple of thousand here, lots of smaller amounts there, and very occasional gifts of as much as $10,000. We once raised more than $20,000 at a glittering dinner/performance in the Hilton, and several Helpmann initiatives we dreamed up in those days remain as good as anything else in Australia, and better than most. So many young people got new opportunities from Helpmann; grants, mentorships, prizes, access to famous visiting artists, and even residencies overseas. It wasn't the grand affair envisaged in the late 1980s, and it wasn't rattling competitor institutions anywhere else in the art education world, but it was pretty good. And one of my perennial favourites has been the jazz awards I was describing above.

Jazz has been in my life from my first memories, because of Dad. He was a good pianist, mainly in jazz forms but also trying his hand at the classics. A family legend was that Mum and Dad had to sell his Bechstein grand piano when she was expecting me, because they needed the space in their small house in Scotland. As a teenager, he had dreamed of playing in a jazz big band, and he managed to get one gig when the piano player in a Glasgow outfit got sick. To his horror, he realised almost instantly they began rehearsing that he was nowhere near good enough to fit in smoothly, and he didn't even ask if he could play with them again.

The connections he had made had one great result however. In August 1938, Fats Waller came to Glasgow, for one night only. Dad got the job of being Fats' minder for a whole day of rehearsals. Most of the songs we were listening to on records twenty years later, he heard live that day: 'I Can't Give You Anything But Love', 'Honeysuckle Rose' (Dad's favourite), 'The Joint Is Jumping', 'Your Feets' Too Big' and my favourite, 'Two Sleepy People'. He had to stand near the piano while Fats played, and keep his gin glass topped up. A whole bottle of Gordons was consumed, but Dad didn't find out till much later what the frequent trips to the toilet were about. Fats snorted many lines, was full of gin, and yet kept on playing and singing, in my dad's words, 'like an angel'. Again, Dad's self-esteem as a pianist took a big hit. For the rest of his life, he wrestled with the deceptive intricacies of 'Honeysuckle Rose', but drunk or sober, he just knew he never came close to the casual artistry of Fats Waller. I thought Dad sounded great, but there was no way into his damaged psyche on that topic.

With music so central to my happiness, one of my chief delights about being in the Helpmann Academy was that my office was adjacent to the rehearsal spaces for the jazz students. Listening to some of the first-years was a bit tedious, but when they were final-year and honours students, it was like being in a nightclub all day long.

In 1994, my dad was in a nursing home, dementia having long finished off whatever comfort he had enjoyed from playing a piano. One day that year, I sat still in the office for an hour or more, as a gifted student – I never saw who – worked hard to get 'Honeysuckle Rose' right on the piano in the room next door. I was trying to write a report, but I had to give up and just drown in the beauty of the piece and the images of my father. That young musician would never have known of the middle-aged man in the room next door, sitting very still, misty-eyed and lost in memories.

With the twenty-fifth anniversary of the academy pending, I've been reflecting on those days, filled with hope, adventures among the rich and famous, some despairing moments, but many more of pure pleasure. For a variety of reasons, I moved on to another job in 1997. It was partly due to some major own-goals in my personal life, and partly a sense that this wasn't my true vocation. Of course, I had loved helping a prodigiously talented young pianist get to the Prague competition, a violinist win a scholarship to Julliard in New York, or a group of visual arts students to work with their counterparts in Yogyakarta. I read last week that since that time, more than 5,000 students have won those grants, awards, residencies, exchanges and other extra chances to shorten the long odds against success in the art of their choice. It's not a bad record, even if it's not the game-changer I was hoping for.

But it was time to move on. Young offenders, abused children, marginalised homeless people, men and women struggling with mental illness; these and others have always been my natural element. A real job for me was helping underpowered battlers fighting stigma, rejection and ham-fisted efforts to deliver health and welfare services when and where they needed them. In the next few years, after a brief and unhappy stint as an arts consultant, I was privileged to get several great opportunities doing just that.

Not a Fokker Friendship

'Nobody is to say anything about Fokker Friendships.'

I was walking across the floor of a vast aircraft hangar in Bandung, one of a group of twenty or so South Australians, guests on a visit approved by Indonesia's vice-president, B.J. Habibie. As director of the Helpmann Academy, I was the sole representative of the arts and culture sector. In front of us was a gleaming new plane, which looked, well, exactly like a Fokker Friendship.

Our group leader, an Adelaide communications consultant who was president of the Australia-Indonesia Business Council, was speaking very quietly. 'OK, it's based on aspects of the Fokker design, but we are instructed that this is a revolutionary new version specifically adapted to south-east Asian conditions, a truly Indonesian aircraft. Please show your appreciation at the right moments.'

Walking with us, surrounding us really, were several soldiers, all carrying automatic weapons. They were unsmiling, moving with the catlike grace of very fit men, herding us towards the plane, which we gathered was the only thing we were meant to be looking at in this very secure weapons manufacturing complex. I couldn't help noticing the endless rows of cannon shells, and belts filled with ammunition, some of which I feared would be used against Ambonese, Achinese, West Papuan and East Timorese freedom fighters and civilians.

Unlike B.J. Habibie, who died just recently, I'm not an engineer, so there may well have been revolutionary new technology all around us as we stepped into the plane. But, as someone who had flown in them many times, all I could see and smell was a very new, spotless replica of a Fokker Friendship. We moved along the aisle, murmuring banal appreciation, trying to think of something to say. Somebody asked our on-board guide whether the plane was in service yet.

'Very soon, very soon.'

'Has it flown yet?'

'Very soon, very soon.'

I can't remember the name given to the plane, but I can find no references to it today, so I assume this was another project that went on to the back-burner in the tumult at the end of the Suharto regime, only months after our visit in 1996. But on that day, we all smiled, and told our tour guide how marvellous it looked, and did our best to look impressed in a knowledgeable sort of way.

Outside the hangar, the heat was intense. Hectares of open concrete, criss-crossed by groups of soldiers marching in formation, and military vehicles moving at high speed completed a scene that belonged in a James Bond movie, where the enormity of the fiendish genius's headquarters is revealed. Like Bond, some of us were wondering if we were going to be let out of there.

Back on the bus, somebody started to say loudly that it was a Fokker Friendship, realising just in time that the Indonesian guide was on board, and ending with a lame phrase about how looks can deceive.

The bus stopped outside another building. We were marshalled into an enormous conference room, and asked to take our places at a U-shaped arrangement of tables and chairs, facing a more imposing desk and chair at the end of the room. We sweated, drank our water, and waited. A nervous frisson was pervasive.

Our delegation's leader sat down beside me. 'I'm going to say a few words thanking our hosts, and then I'd like you to be one of the people giving a short presentation. Is that OK with you?'

I had two questions. First, who would I be presenting to? And second, was I supposed to know before this about a presentation? I hadn't prepared anything.

'Well, we don't know just yet, but I gather it's a very important person from the government. And you'll be fine, David, you always speak well.'

I was tense, making a few notes, but confident I could carry this off. I was distracted by a disturbance, as about twenty more soldiers, these ones all spit-and-polished perfection, carrying automatic weapons, trotted into the room and stood at ease along the walls behind us all. 'At ease' meaning legs apart, blank stares, looking anything but relaxed, rifles across their torso, apparently ready for any threats we might pose.

Then Vice-President Habibie himself, looking tiny among his bodyguards, strode in and stood by his desk. We jumped up, and waited until he sat down. For a moment, as he looked around the room at all of us, beaming, there was silence, then he welcomed us to Indonesia, and to the IPTN complex. He spoke first in Indonesian, then briefly in English, with a high-pitched voice full of enthusiasm.

Our tour leader replied briefly, then turned to me. 'Your excellency, I will now ask several members of our delegation to speak briefly about their specific interests in partnerships between Indonesia and South Australia. May I first introduce Mr David Meldrum, whose work is in arts education.'

No warning. My first thought was something like 'You bastard'. Then I was somewhere beyond fear, in that cold, silent place I can go to in moments of crisis. Habibie and the tour leader were both looking at me intently with expectant smiles, and for a few long seconds my mind was a blank.

There is a lovely Scottish word that my father often used: 'blethering'. To blether is to waffle, and I willed myself to start out with something as crisp and as non-blethering as possible. It was words like these. (I have no notes, only memory.)

'Your excellency, arts and culture are every bit as important to both our countries as the heavy industry, defence, health and other technologies that we will talk about today. Australia and Indonesia have much to offer each other. In fact, we already exchange ideas and work together in many artistic and cultural endeavours. This enriches us all. I hope to cement new partnerships in arts education that will build on this foundation. Thank you again for this opportunity.'

Habibie's smile did not waver, and with no comment he looked to our leader to point to the next speaker. I leaned back, my body buzzing, and breathed. It was someone else's turn.

I was just beginning to study Bahasa Indonesia, so I listened closely to Habibie each time he spoke, before the interpreters' version, trying to follow at least a bit of it. As we heard about housing, agriculture, joint mining ventures and information technology, he caught my eye several times. I sat it out with a bland smile, assuming it was because of my seating position at the head of the U-shape, facing him directly.

Then he concluded a brief conversation with one of our speakers, saying, 'I don't think our speaker from the arts needs to wait for the translation.'

He thought I was following his every word. I smiled a little more warmly, and got away with it. He turned to the next speaker and made no other comment. Our tour leader expressed surprise afterwards, not realising I was so fluent. When I explained that I had about twenty words at my command, even he thought I was just being modest. I left it at that, and managed to avoid any interpreting duties for the rest of the tour.

One of our delegates should have earned a medal for bravery. I think she was an obstetrician, and she was talking about infant mortality. Habibie interrupted her to ask if she was suggesting Indonesia had a problem in this area. She gave him both barrels, explaining that a baby was something like thirty times more likely to die in their first year of life in Indonesia, as compared to Australia. The figure for death and disability of birthing mothers was equally shocking.

Habibie's smile disappeared. There was silence as he looked down, cupping his hands below his chin. Our tour leader looked stricken. The obstetrician's face was reddening. I looked to the soldiers; to my fevered imagination, they looked even more alert.

Habibie looked up. He beamed again. 'Bravo. We need to hear information on important matters like this, even if it is uncomfortable.

I want you to meet with my senior health officials at the first opportunity. Thank you for being so frank.'

The meeting ended shortly after, with an equally intimidating display of military efficiency involving coming to attention, turning to the left and marching out after the vice-president. We all breathed a little easier, joking now about how scary it had been to be a presenter. I went out to the toilets, and found the obstetrician standing alone in a hallway. When I congratulated her, she told me she had just thrown up in the women's restroom. She had been fighting nausea since that interaction with Habibie, determined not to show any signs of distress. Even now, she was struggling for composure, knowing I would be the first of many wanting to talk with her. We stood quietly for a minute or two, then she took a deep breath and headed back into the conference room.

The trip on the bus back to our hotel was just as dramatic as when we came to the complex. That morning we had been greeted by two motorcyclist police officers, both with Hollywood-star looks and huge smiles, immaculate in black leathers and sunglasses. They had ushered us on to the bus, then mounted their black bikes, revving the motors loudly before taking off at high speed. The streets of Bandung were crowded with cars, bicycles, trucks and other buses, moving slowly. But the crowd had parted as we approached at what I think was about sixty kilometres an hour, with the sirens wailing. I'd jumped in the bus first, so I could sit in the front seat beside the driver. I watched the many near misses with horrified fascination, feeling embarrassed to be part of this blunt display of official power.

On the return trip, as we hurtled across downtown Bandung, I sat at the back, on my own. In front of me, many of my colleagues were talking excitedly about big-money opportunities that seemed to dangle in easy reach. Thousands of prefab houses to be built, thousands of students to educate, dozens of bridges and other massive infrastructure projects ready to start. Just pay the ten to fifteen per cent 'project acquisition fees' – that is, the bribes – and the millions would flow.

I didn't like the situation at all. Many of the delegates were hoping to be carpet-baggers, rushing in to this underdeveloped country where most people were poor, while their rulers; politicians, generals and police commanders; were bizzarely rich. We – I hoped with the exception of myself and the obstetrician – were white guys looking for a share of the action, laughing about the corruption and looking away from the exploitation involved. But I knew I was complicit in this corrupt game, from the moment I agreed to say nothing about the plane that wasn't supposed to be a Fokker Friendship. My offsider at the Helpmann Academy had often told me I would go to the opening of an envelope. I usually saw it as my job, but this was one invitation I should never have accepted.

Bad Job Choice

I knew it was time to leave the Helpmann Academy, but the job offers for me in my preferred fields of health and welfare services just weren't there. Late in 1997, the Liberal Party was back in power, and the new Minister of Health had been opposition leader during the Hillcrest Hospital dramas of five years before. I gathered I was still regarded with some caution at least. I probably should have stuck it out in the Academy until something good came up, but my personal life was in chaos right at that moment. When I was offered a job reviewing public subsidies for arts institutions, I grabbed it without really checking out what I was supposed to achieve. By the time I did, it was too late to turn back.

The new CEO of the Arts Department was an economic conservative, who had assured his minister that substantial budget cuts were possible without much political risk. In our first discussion, he made several key points, namely:

> Most of the senior people in the State Theatre, the Festival Centre, State Opera, Art Galley of SA, et cetera, et cetera, were 'socialist types' who were too used to the easy life of government funding without much accountability for results.

> They weren't trying nearly hard enough to raise funds from the private sector and the public; if this was the USA, they would have to find most of their income from foundations and the like.

> It was time for a shake-up, so some amalgamations or other forms of restructuring were needed to create opportunities to make the 'fat cats' apply for their own jobs.

> My job included finding substantial savings, beginning with at least a few hundred thousand dollars in the next financial year.

I was very uncomfortable. I had a sinking feeling that this guy would only get more strident and opinionated as we went along, and in other circumstances I would have walked away. But I had just separated from my wife, and I had to prioritise holding on to my public sector executive rank and salary, so that she and my kids would be OK financially. I'd already left the Helpmann Academy a few days before, and there was no going back. This time, I had to take a job I didn't want, the only time I can remember doing that. I asked how long I had to complete what was really a consultancy, and he suggested six months. I agreed and we shook hands.

It was near Christmas, so I had a couple of weeks off, time spent mainly finding somewhere to live, before I had to begin learning how the top end of the subsidised arts world worked. After moving into a friend's house in Semaphore, it was back to the office. Within a short time, I had the walls covered in organisation charts, showing the people and the dollars, which were much less than I had imagined. I think there was less than $20 million in total for the twelve major organisations; and this was in South Australia, which prided itself on being the 'Festival State' because of events including the Adelaide Festival of Arts, the Fringe Festival and the world music event WOMAD, which were, and still are, much celebrated in Australia.

There had been several other reviews in the couple of years before this, both of individual organisations and of arts funding in general. I had to read them all, and there was little there to support the government's current downsizing objectives. I don't know for sure if this had anything to do with it, but during that consultancy, the Arts Minister was the only member of the Liberal government I ever saw at an arts event of any type, except for one performance of *The Pirates of Penzance*, where I met the Minister of Health. The arts just wasn't their scene, although I must say the Arts Minister was and still is a stalwart supporter of many art forms, so I think the fiscal pressure was coming from other cabinet colleagues, most likely the Treasurer. My guess is she was a lonely voice in that cabinet, not least because she was the only woman.

For about three months, I prepared an overall summary of where the money was, how it was being spent, and how that all looked in comparison to other parts of Australia. It soon became obvious that South Australia was not providing any more public funds than anyone else, but the proportion of income raised from other sources was low compared to New South Wales and Victoria. One woman, a rich arts donor, told me our problem was that 'Adelaide doesn't have enough wealthy Jews. In Sydney, and especially in Melbourne, they are the backbone of the arts.' Whatever the truth of that, I knew from my time in the Helpmann Academy that getting large donations and bequests for the arts was rare in Adelaide. I had so nearly proved otherwise with the Helpmann fortune, but nearly changes nothing. It was all very well to say the local subsidised bodies weren't trying hard enough, but their boards were stacked with conservative, well-connected people, many appointed by the current government, and they didn't seem to have the answers.

My only recourse was to look at achieving some administrative savings by reducing the number of separate arts organisations. I had observed before what I think of as the iron law of separateness – organisations will tend to want to remain separate, unless there is a major incentive to change, or force is applied. CEOs and board members work in their little corner of the world because they love it, and there needs to be a very good reason for them to lurch into the unknown. As I got to know all the CEOs of these arts agencies, I could see no signs of an appetite for new arrangements, except for those few who told me 'strictly between you and me' that they would be happy to absorb one or more of the others as long as they retained the lead role.

I bargained with the Arts CEO. How much did we actually have to save in the 1998–99 financial year? We eventually settled on $200,000, and I started devising scenarios that would achieve this. Was anything definitely off the table? The answer was 'No, but you'd be crazy to touch organisation X, or Y, or Z.' With few options left, I proposed two major amalgamations, both leaving one of the untouchables in charge and enlarged, which would yield $200,000. (Based on experience, I actually meant 'Just might yield $200,000, with exceptional luck and steady management', but consultants don't say that sort of thing.)

The CEO was impressed, and surprised. What I suggested was 'doable' (his term) as long as we kept it a secret until the minister was onside. I was to write it all up, prepare a one-page summary for the minister, and say nothing to anyone else in the department. I could then wind up my consultancy, and make my own arrangements to find other employment. Within a week, I delivered, and waited to be called to the minister's office, the usual next step in these things.

I'd done what was asked of me. I knew these changes would need very adroit political manoeuvring to have any chance, especially given some of the heavy-hitters on the boards of the organisations who would think of themselves as losers. I intended to say that to the minister that when I saw her, and offer to assist. I liked her, and I didn't want to see her get further marginalised among her more conservative and minimally arts-loving colleagues. But the call never came.

Somebody must have leaked. The minister was confronted by journalists asking if it was true that a secret report existed; one that proposed to cut funding to iconic arts organisations. I thought she had received my briefing, because the Arts Department CEO had told me he handed it over personally. In retrospect, it's just possible she was blindsided. I'm sure she said the usual things, such as 'We are always looking closely at how taxpayers' dollars are spent, but no decisions have been made about any cuts of the type you describe.' The journalists, obviously holding a copy of my report, pressed harder, but she managed to fend them off. I would be surprised if phone calls from irate board members didn't come in thick and fast.

I knew none of this. It happened a couple of weeks after I had finished that job, and I was just beginning a new role in the Health Department. Today's constant newsfeed on the smartphone didn't exist then, and I didn't often watch the evening news. It wasn't till the day after the minister's run-in with journalists that a friend told me what had happened in the Legislative Council the night before. The minister told the council that she had just been made aware of 'The Meldrum Report', which 'contained some rather radical ideas about restructuring the main arts bodies'. 'But', she went on, 'it is certainly not my intention to implement any of these proposals.'

Which dropped me right in it. My first call was to the Arts Department CEO, but he never, and I mean never, got back to me. I wrote to the minister, and got no reply. I was very stirred up, worried that my name would be mud in the arts world from now on. And it was, at least with people who didn't know me well. Within a week, one board I was on asked me to leave the room, while they discussed a vote of no confidence in me. This was brought on by a fellow board member who happened to be CEO of one of the arts agencies I had recommended should be amalgamated with another. The vote was upheld; I returned to the meeting to be informed so. I was frostily thanked by the chairman, and asked to go. I gave a little speech, to a sea of thin lips, thanking them for the opportunity to support their work, and left in as dignified a manner as I could dredge up. The next few days were very hard for me.

Although I kept quiet, lots of people guessed correctly what had happened, and I didn't lose any good friends. Ironically, because the arts world is so marginal to most people's interests, almost nobody in the health/welfare world had even noticed. Which was great, because I didn't want to deal with a reputation as a victim or a loser. As usual, I preferred to move on, even though I did feel wounded for a while. Some enmities persisted. The CEO of one arts company refused to speak with me ever again, whisking past me in the street or at events with exuberant disdain. But I could live with that. I was just doing my job; I was told funding cuts had to happen, and the proposals I made were the least damaging ones I could come up with. As for the Arts Minister, the CEO had told her significant savings were feasible without much political risk. He was wrong. So be it.

Recently, Charmaine and I went to a fascinating talk on Japanese art from the seventeenth century. And there was the Arts Minister concerned, now long retired. We chatted easily, and I enjoyed her company for a few minutes. Those events in 1998 all seemed so unimportant now. We were just actors in a process of a type that goes on constantly. I know I did my best, and It's likely she feels the same way about herself.

Teeth At Risk

In 1999, I did a short stint as CEO of the South Australian Community Housing Authority, while the agency's future was being reviewed. The previous CEO had left under a bit of a cloud, so a 'steady hand' was needed for six months or so. It was fun, and the mission to deliver housing for low-income people certainly fitted my values, but a bigger challenge came along sooner than I expected.

Another CEO had fallen out with his board of directors and resigned, but this time the conservative Liberal Party government was talking about winding up a whole public health agency – an icon of progressive healthcare, the South Australian Dental Service, known to all as SADS. Private dentists had long argued that they could do all the dental work for school-age children and poor people with improved subsidies, and that there was no need for salaried dentists to be employed as public servants. The Australian Dental Association, really the private dentists' lobby group, had the ear of the Health Minister. The end of SADS was a serious possibility, when the Human Services Department chief executive persuaded her minister that installing a 'troubleshooter' CEO for twelve months was worth a try. My name was put forward, and I thought that might scuttle things, because the Health Minister and I had a chequered history, dating back to my role in closing a mental hospital.

A Liberal Party elder statesman was sent to see me, to suss me out. He was extremely blunt, telling me that he agreed with the private dentists, and that I'd have a hard job convincing him that 'a pack of chardonnay socialist public servants' could do a better job than private enterprise. He looked at my CV, we talked for quite a while, and he decided that it was worth a try, as long as he became a board member, 'to keep an eye on you', and that I undertook to (a) get the budget back into balance within six months and (b) 'get the Australian Dental Association and that professor of dentistry from Adelaide University to both stop bothering the minister and premier with a string of complaints about SADS'. I do like a clear brief, and I said I'd take on the job.

The chair of the board, a recent government appointment, was a private dentist, and he shared with me early on that he had real doubts about winding up SADS. His best guess was that there was no way his colleagues could do the amount of dentistry required for the same cost. In other words, privatising this public service would most likely cost taxpayers more. But I knew from several politically sensitive previous jobs that the facts are weak in the face of ideology and party platforms, so this was going to be about really good information at my fingertips, a quick return to budget discipline and building solid relationships with the main complainers.

The honeymoon period in any change leadership job is extremely valuable, and I tried not to waste it. I shook a lot of hands, talked to many meetings of staff, and called up briefing papers on every topic that seemed related to SADS losing so much political capital that it had nearly been closed down. The board, at least half of them Liberal Party stalwarts, several apparently complicit in disseminating damaging stories about SADS, were my first target for spreading the love. I had one-on-one meetings with nearly all of them within the first few weeks. It was quickly obvious that a balanced budget would give me some breathing room to assemble more good news about SADS' value, so that became the top priority.

It took several heated management meetings, and complete rejigging of financial reporting, to clarify that we were heading for a deficit of about $2.5 million by the end of the financial year, less than nine months away. With a total annual spend of $35 million, most tied up in salaries and essential dental supplies, this was a scary assignment.

None of my senior colleagues thought it could be done. But we did it, over six weeks of analysis, debate and difficult decisions. Workloads were increased, periods between scheduled dental check-ups were extended, stockpiling of dental supplies was refined to 'just in time', capital works projects were deferred or spread over more years, vacancies in non-essential areas were left unfilled, leases were renegotiated and more dentistry was farmed out to private dentists willing to accept our low rates. No patient was going to miss out on urgent care, we sacked nobody, but we were going to break even. The board were satisfied, and we had the temporary reprieve we needed to start working towards a better future.

I think my management team surprised themselves with this achievement. What they didn't know was that I was amazed. This was the most serious bit of cost-cutting I had ever attempted, by far, and my confident demeanour in the first few weeks was more about hope than certainty. Patient, detailed, sometimes gruelling dissection of every spending line gradually yielded up a clear path to survival. It was exhilarating. We had come up with an austerity budget that hurt nobody.

While all this was under way, I was getting to know the 'stakeholders' of dentistry, or oral health as it was becoming known. The Australian Dental Association, which had a fearsome reputation as a lobby group, was quite easy to work with. My predecessor had stayed right away from them, but I asked for their help on several matters, especially finding dentists who would take on some of our work at our rates. They did this quickly and graciously, and seemed to thrive on being asked at last. Together with the professor of dentistry mentioned above, we worked out a scheme for private country dentists to provide placements for final-year dental students. This had been on the back-burner for years, and country people were being denied the extra services that these young trainees delivered under supervision. It was so easy to arrange, and now the board had the first of the good news stories that I thought might save SADS. The Liberal Party elder statesman, whose constituency was in the country, was delighted. The

SADS whisperers in the corridors of power were starting to say the right things.

Dentists, and the dental therapists, hygienists, prosthetists and assistants who work with them, were an entirely new type of colleague for me. Their world was a bit narrow, focused on the number of 'teeth at risk' – I kid you not, that was how they measured demand. Most of them had gone directly from high school into the teeth business, and it showed. Except for the specialist dentists, including orthodontists, endodontists, maxillofacial surgeons and others, most were very shy outside of the oral health world, a bit defensive around medical doctors, and convinced that nobody else could understand their work. Although many were long-serving senior people, they had minimal networks in the bureaucracy and politics of government, which helps explain how they had failed to see the dangers I was brought in to deal with.

The dental therapists were an unusual lot in several ways. They had mostly been recruited about fifteen years before, in a scheme to bring dentistry to all primary school children at an affordable cost to the taxpayer. They were trained to a level where they could do inspection and cleaning of all teeth, and extractions and fillings on milk teeth in younger children. Along with fluoridation of water, the School Dental Scheme was credited with giving South Australian children the equal-lowest rate (along with Norway, I think) of tooth decay in the world. Private dentists were apoplectic about this threat to their monopoly at the time the scheme began, and they fought successfully against any further recruitment. They were still making scurrilous remarks about the limited value of therapists when I came along.

The other unusual thing, besides this one cohort all being women and about the same age – thirty-five to forty when I knew them – was that they all seemed to be very good-looking. I think one or two of them had been Miss South Australia contestants around the time they came into the scheme. I was told later that one of my predecessors had managed the whole selection process, which was swamped with applicants, and he had used his power to fill his working world with beautiful women. If that is true, I can only wonder how many other talented people, men and women, might have come into that scheme if they'd had the chance.

And, like most of their oral health colleagues, all of them had perfect teeth. Before this job, I had never really noticed teeth much, although I was self-conscious that mine were a bit battered and small. Within a few months of being in SADS, I was planning my own major upgrade, at considerable cost. Sitting in meetings where everybody had a Hollywood smile does that to you.

A friend of mine was and still is a very successful private dentist, and he had been telling me for some time that the upfront 'mates rates' he was offering me were trivial compared to a lifetime of comfortable eating and a confident smile. Now I was ready.

He said, 'If you bought a new car, within a few months you would have forgotten how much it cost – it will be the same with this.' I had the feeling it wasn't my new car we were talking about, although he did tell me he fixed my teeth at cost price.

Over the next year, SADS became the poster child of the health system in many ways; reducing waiting lists, working pretty much harmoniously with private dentistry and their professional association, and, most importantly, not blowing its budget. We were given extra funding to reduce country waiting lists, and we delivered all of that through private dentists. I involved all of the staff who wanted to participate in a strategic planning process; focusing the priorities for the next few years. It was very satisfying, particularly as I watched jaded people start to get excited about their work.

A few remained grumpily uninvolved. There was a professor who told me, 'Don't interfere in my services unless you want me to withdraw them.' He ran a public clinic on our behalf. People were told they had a morning appointment or an afternoon appointment. This meant waiting for hours, often to be told to come back tomorrow. I challenged him about it, and he said, 'These people would just be sitting at home watching daytime TV – they're better off here.' I stayed in his face until he compromised and divided the day into four sessions. I hate those attitudes to people doing it tough, and luckily almost all the SADS professionals felt the same way as me.

With a new strategic plan, a budget that we all knew could work, and a supportive board, we had managed to get fully on-side with the Liberal Party-led government, especially the Health Minister. By now he and i had a good working relationship, which developed further through several professional connections for the next fifteen years.

All this good cheer turned out to be just in time to see them get kicked out of government in an election that brought Labor back into power. I found it ironic that this whole change-management process, under threat of closure, would most likely never have happened if Labor had been running things all along, but they were delighted to give SADS a small budget increase, and take the credit for saving the public dental service. All's well that ends well…and so on.

My tenure as CEO was short-lived. The new Minister of Health said to me privately that 'We might use you for some other projects we have in mind.' I wouldn't have minded staying with SADS a bit longer, to see the new plan unfold, but it wasn't to be. The nation's best dental administrator, who was running the Victorian equivalent of SADS, wanted to come home, and he took over from me shortly after that chat with the minister.

My next 'troubleshooter CEO' job was great, but I have some very happy memories from the time I ran the dental services. For the first time in my life, most days I had felt fairly confident that I knew what I was doing; that the processes I was leading, and the understandings I could call on to back my judgements, were generally about right. I'd learned to be patient, and to be a better listener, and it was working. And I still have those new teeth. As my dentist friend said at the time, 'Only the best for the boss of SADS.'

Up In Flames

On 27 April 2001, during the time I was CEO of SADS, our house in Torrens Park burnt down. Charmaine and I and our house guest got out unhurt, but almost all our possessions were lost.

I'd come back from a plane trip to rural South Australia that evening, arranging country placements for dental students; a project that was a huge success. So we had a late, cheerful meal with a friend who was catching a plane back to the US in the morning. She had just done some washing, and it was too damp to pack, so we set up the clothes airer in front of the gas heater. At about ten, she was still packing and repacking (always a puzzle to me, this repacking: I just fold it, flatten it and sit on the case to close it – easy) so we said goodnight and went to bed. Charmaine was soon asleep, but I read on until just before eleven. I could hear J (I won't use her name) moving around in her room above as I started to nod off.

Sometime later, maybe only a few minutes, a distant but piercing electronic sound slowly registered with me. The oven? A phone? Charmaine woke and said, 'Something's beeping.'

I got up groggily to check it out, and as I turned into the hallway I saw a bright glow coming under the door to the living area. It still didn't compute – I can't recall what I was thinking – but I opened the door to look straight into hell. Half the lounge room was already on fire, and J was standing on the stairs screaming. Her damp clothes were disappearing in the flames. She had shifted the airer closer to the fire to get them to dry faster so she could finish packing.

In the next few seconds, I realised the fire was likely to act like a bomb if the gas pipe to the heater melted. I yelled to Charmaine to get up and out as fast as she could. We stood in the front door, looking around for what we could grab, but decided we had to get away right then. We ran out of the house with nothing, and up the driveway. We turned to look as the lounge room windows glowed brighter, then, after maybe a minute, there was a huge explosion and the fire raced upstairs as far as the upper-storey roof in seconds. Charmaine and I stood in silence, her holding down her only garment, a T-shirt, while our guest cried and talked non-stop in her shock and guilt.

Very soon, the fire reached the cars parked in our driveway. Charmaine had recently bought a beautiful old Mercedes 280, immaculate, and the first car she had ever owned that had really excited her. We said she didn't drive to places; she proceeded. Now we watched as the bonnet paint blistered and blackened, then the windscreen cracked open, letting the flames in to begin consuming the whole interior. Somehow it was our horrified focus for a while. The rest of the house was on fire, but we stared in disbelief as the Mercedes disintegrated.

From somewhere, neighbours, an ambulance and the fire brigade had surrounded us within about five minutes. Kind people gave Charmaine more clothes and the paramedics concentrated on calming our by-now hysterical guest. They also tried to get Charmaine to rest inside the ambulance, and she had to refuse adamantly before they would let her be. The firefighters said they didn't need an emergency call; one of them had seen the flames from the station about two kilometres away and knew they had to hurry.

This gets personal. I withdrew into an unreachable place, as I sometimes do in a major crisis. Eyes glued to the fire, I heard little of what was being said to me, and with the paramedics so engaged, I stopped thinking about how Charmaine and J were doing. I know more about this behaviour of mine nowadays; my retreating from any surface emotion under extreme pressure. Its roots are in some nasty stuff when I was a boy. It's a two-edged sword – I can be a calm rock to people wanting leadership when the shit hits the fan, but fail the people I love when they need me most. I think I have moved on, but that night, its grip on me was unbreakable. After maybe fifteen cold, lonely minutes, I began to feel I had to reach out to someone, and I chose to ring my daughter. I should say that we had been almost completely estranged for several years, with occasional awkward visits our only contact. I can't remember the phone conversation, but she said she would come over straight away. Within what seemed minutes, she was there, holding me tightly. She was the bridge from my frozen shock back to the present, so I could turn my attention again to Charmaine and our guest.

I found J was being taken home by our friend Jenny, where she stayed for a few days. We stood and watched the blaze wordlessly, until we agreed we had to focus on what to do now. Charmaine rang her friend Lynne and she came to collect us soon after. The fire was nearly under control, the Mercedes was a blackened ruin, and most of the house was gone. All this in less than an hour since we heard the smoke alarm. We had a bed for the night, and kept Len and Lynne up for a couple of hours, talking non-stop until the adrenalin ran out and we collapsed into sleep.

Next day we went back, and our new reality kicked in. To enter where the front door had been, we had to get around the grotesque skeleton of the Mercedes. All our clothes, books, CDs, paintings and furniture were damaged beyond repair or completely gone. All that remained of the billiard table was some blackened wood and the brass of the pockets. Nearly all of Charmaine's photos, kids' paintings and academic records were ash. Most sobering were the two bedrooms of Charmaine's girls, Liv and Kate. They spent every alternate week with us, and were staying with their dad the night before. Their rooms upstairs were destroyed, and it was obvious they would have had great difficulty escaping, with the stairs on fire and no easy way out over the roof. That may just be the best bit of luck they, and we, will ever have.

We picked over the few things that looked salvageable, and put them in suitcases that later stank so badly they had to be dumped. Everything we owned now fitted into the back seat and boot of a loan car I had. This wasn't my first time; when I left my marriage a couple of years before, I had just a bootful of belongings. But for Charmaine it was much, much harder. She had saved so many belongings from the stages of her life, as a girl, a young nurse, an academic and a mother. Almost everything was gone.

We had only been in this house for nine months, and the previous owner dropped in while we were sifting the debris. He checked that we were all right, then wandered around the scene looking increasingly grim. He was an engineer, and he and his wife had put decades of effort into extending, renovating and equipping that house. Everything about the place worked so well, and it was mainly down to him. He hadn't really wanted to leave, but there was some imperative I can't recall. The house had been his pride and joy for more than thirty years, and now it was a blackened, stinking ruin. In my bewildered state, I felt his loss as keenly as my own.

The next few days drifted by in a hazy, not quite real way. We both went back to work; we found a house to rent short-term with the help of the insurers; both Kate and I had birthday parties. We told our story again and again, and the shock began to loosen its grip. We took our house guest to the airport, stopping for a quiet beach walk where we made sure she knew we held no grudges. My colleagues at SADS were wonderful. One took me aside gently one day to tell me my efforts to get the smell out of my suits was a failure – I had to throw them away. I felt pretty upbeat; we had survived intact, and we were going to move on OK.

But a week later, I was walking along a busy street to a SADS meeting I was going to chair, and without warning, I felt overwhelmed. I stood against a building, breathing hard, fighting off tears, and I knew I couldn't do my job. I rang my offsider and told him I just couldn't manage today.

He said, 'Mate, It's about time. Don't come in till you're ready.' That one-liner was the only PTSD counselling I sought or received, and it helped me enormously.

Another friend sent me a message a few days later. It was a quote from an ancient Chinese text: 'Now that my house has burnt down, I can see the moon rising.' And it was mainly true. We were off on our next adventure, thinking about where to live, buying lots of essential items like wine, paintings and CDs, and pulling together as a team after this joint, shocking experience. That was our 'moon rising'. Another was a new closeness with my daughter. We spoke often after the fire, and that continues: an enduring joy for me and an unexpected bonus from that night.

One man I knew at the top end of the public service rang me a couple of weeks later, apologising profusely because he had just found out about our misfortune, to ask if there was any way he could help. Usually in these situations you say, 'No, but thanks for asking.' This time I said I was concerned that we would be paying two lots of stamp duty in twelve months if we bought a new house soon. The figure was something like $30,000. I knew there was a provision in the rules for waiving the duty in 'exceptional circumstances'. Could he consider if this situation fitted that description? He said he would look into it, but I could hear the distinct note of cooling compassion. I never heard from him again. Ah well, it was worth a try.

Losing so many possessions can be cleansing – most of it turns out to be unimportant. A few really special, personal things can leave wounds, and you may not know what they are till it happens, but you do heal gradually. I still miss that house, though. Charmaine and I bought it together not long after we found each other. We snuggled in there in a sort of dream state, like adolescents discovering a new life. Someone bought the shell, and rebuilt it over the next couple of years. We went to the open inspection, and it was lovely, but not the place we had lived in.

I thought of writing this recently. I walked into a city office, and on one whole wall was a 1970s wallpaper picture of a forest in autumn. It was exactly the one that faced you when you came in the front door of that house. Seventeen years on, I reacted immediately, then stopped and composed myself. I had a meeting to go to. Memories and the emotions that go with them are indelible, but life goes on.

Whatever It Takes

I've been reading about the L'Hopital General, a very old building in the small city of Uzes where we stayed not long ago, on a cycling tour around Provence. It was established in 1214 as a 'hospital for the poor, thanks to a generous donation'. Most of its functions were convalescence, a place to die quietly, or isolation when infectious disease was about. In 1720, almost all of its patients and staff were killed by the plague, so no one went near the place for decades.

The story set me thinking about my own brief foray into a modern attempt to keep people out of hospital, unless they really needed to be there. I was the first and only CEO of the Advanced Community Care Association, begun in 2003 and voluntarily wound up by administrators in 2006. During 2002, our enthusiastic Minister of Health had announced a 'Generational Review', a 'root and branch analysis' of the health system in South Australia. I was brought in as one of a number of senior people who would hold consultations, sift the evidence and write position papers on how services could and should change. Unfortunately, it degenerated into a very expensive talkfest followed by fiddling with the organisation charts, none of which actually promised to give anyone a better health outcome. Within a few months, I was desperate for a real job, somewhere I could improve the experience and survival chances of actual people dealing with serious health issues.

An old friend rang me out of the blue, suggesting I apply to run the newly formed Advanced Community Care Association (ACCA), an NGO created by three leading community health organisations. Their three CEOs had got together to see how they could reduce what they saw as widespread unnecessary hospitalisation. They had already managed to talk the government into giving them a small grant to provide care to people in aged care facilities as an alternative to a trip to hospital. Two phone calls, one interview, and within about a week, I had the job.

I started with just a desk, a phone and a small budget. I recruited two colleagues who had the skills and networks I needed for ACCA to have an impact in the system. There was a lot of reading and talking to do, in an effort to get up to speed with current practice, evidence of what did and didn't work, and at what comparative cost. I quickly encountered the basic conundrum that hampers these programs. A Treasury official told me coolly, 'Your new program will only interest us if hospital beds close as a result – and that will never happen.' In general, history since then, in Australia at least, has proved him right.

So I decided early on not to argue that we would save public money, but instead to show that people/patients wanted these new alternatives, and that they were not very expensive to provide. The evidence, from Australia and several other countries, was certainly there. More than ninety per cent of people facing hospital care, if asked whether they would prefer some or all of their care to be at home, say yes, as long as their GP is supportive. This strong preference holds up across gender, socioeconomic status and age, but is routinely ignored, especially in a crisis, resulting in large numbers of people in most hospitals being there more often, and for longer than they need to be.

The ancient hospital in Uzes demonstrated a simple principle: people only went to hospital when there was no acceptable alternative. They knew even then that putting together a lot of people with serious diseases, away from their family and friends, could be a risky proposition, but sometimes poverty and/or the severity of your condition leaves little option. Today, rich countries vie to provide the best hospitals they can, at huge cost, with full support from public opinion. For many conditions and treatments, there are complete or partial alternatives to hospital care, but closing beds to provide home care is still seen as courting political suicide.

In ACCA, we started by getting to know emergency department leaders. Everybody knows many of the people presenting in the ED don't need to be there, and in some cases definitely shouldn't be there because of the health risks involved. It wasn't controversial to ask about who might be candidates for diversion to home care. 'Do something about the psychos and the wrinklies' came up often. Blunt but honest. 'We can't help the psychos and we hate seeing the wrinklies falling apart under the stress of ambulance trips, waiting around on stretchers and getting infections.' Because we had the small grant I mentioned, we decided to have a go at reducing the number of people from aged care homes that were taken to EDs.

It was easy. We advertised to private community nursing agencies, looking for competent people prepared to be on call at short notice when either a GP, a nursing home or a paramedic felt that good nursing care would be a better alternative than a trip to hospital. In the first month, we had about two calls a day to our telephone hotline; within six months it was up to fifty a day. GPs loved the service, because the first thing our call centre operators did was call them and ask for advice about one of their patients. Aged care staff, paramedics and ED staff were all equally enthusiastic. And the private nursing operators were ecstatic about so much new business that they didn't have to chase. Most important, residents and their families spoke highly of this new home care, with wonderful new stories coming in every day.

The disruption and anxiety created by a trip to an ED in an ambulance was only part of the problem we were trying to solve. Even when the health issue is relatively minor to start with, like being dizzy after a fall, or having a cut that needed more than a Band-Aid, when someone who is extremely old and frail comes into a system geared to diagnose and manage all health risks, getting home any time soon is unlikely. OK, sometimes people get lucky when a previously unknown and easily fixable problem is uncovered. Much more commonly, questions lead to tests and more tests, each taking time to arrange, deliver and analyse. Precious time, when an unhappy, anxious person, possibly already coping with some dementia, deteriorates rapidly, sometimes dying within less than a week. It's hard to imagine a more lonely, frightening and confusing way to die than this. Most health professionals agree, but seem incapable of coordinating their activities to stop it happening. We made it easy for them. Call ACCA and someone will be there to provide an alternative within the hour. Whether it was to prevent the trip to hospital, to get them out of the ED, or to get them home a few days earlier, we made it all as easy as a phone call.

The best statistics we could find came from the ambulance service. With their help, we could track the impact of the new program on each aged care facility, on each hospital and even on individual residents over time. Within six months, the overall number of 'carries' from aged care to EDs was down by fifteen per cent. Some patterns began to emerge. For example, some facilities were dramatically more likely to call an ambulance than others; some ten times the average. We began to dig a little deeper, and found these were all privately owned, and known for penny-pinching on staff selection and training. All too often, their policy when a resident had a minor accident or became unwell was 'When in doubt, ship them out'. We offered extra training in first aid and wound management, at no cost to the proprietors. Some took it up, and hospital transfers began to reduce almost immediately. Some turned down the offer because they wanted us to pay for replacement staff while theirs were being trained for a day. We just couldn't bring ourselves to reward that level of selfishness.

The good stories came in thick and fast. One night-duty nurse rang in to say a very old lady had become delirious and paranoid, and was disturbing the other residents. She couldn't do anything, because she was on her own, and couldn't sit with only one of her seventy-five residents for hours. About to call an ambulance, she remembered ACCA, and rang to talk it over. One of our staff asked who the lady trusted most, and it was a cleaner. We asked if the cleaner would be interested in a few hours' overtime to sit with the lady, with us paying.

She was, she did, and within an hour the resident was calm and going to sleep.

A hospital rang with a different problem – one of the famous 'bed-blockers'. These were people who resisted all efforts to leave hospital because they were afraid of or simply didn't want what they were being offered. At a cost of more than $1,000 a day, and people waiting in corridors for a bed, this gave hospital administrators nightmares. This patient was too unwell to go home, was eligible for aged care, but kept refusing to consider the places she was offered. So, on day eighty-eight of her stay in hospital ($88,000 and counting), we visited the lady. She told us immediately that people who ran nursing homes were all dreadful and uncaring. She had arrived at this conclusion by talking with other patients, but had never actually met anyone who worked in such places. She agreed to let us find three in suburbs near her relatives and friends, and get someone from each to visit her. We would pay the aged care facilities for their time. She liked the first person who visited, and asked if she could come back next day to continue the discussion. She did, and they got on wonderfully. With her visitor still there, she called in the ward nurse and told her she would be leaving to live in her new friend's facility as soon as it could be arranged. Face-to-face, caring human contact was all it took. The cost to us was less than $150.

Successes like these meant we were offered more funding to work with anyone, not just aged care residents, who might be able to spend less time, or no time, in hospital with the right community supports. With thousands of people a year using our services, it's hard to select just a few examples that give the flavour of what could be achieved, but here are three.

Bowel preparation

The CEO of an Adelaide hospital rang me to ask if we could take a look at his 'colonoscopy ward'. It turned out that the surgeons involved had a policy that people over seventy-five, living on their own, had to come in the night before, for their 'bowel prep', and stay the next night in case there were any post-procedure complications. Since no other hospital required any inpatient time for such people, and he had a whole ward full staying for two nights, the CEO wondered if I could talk some sense into the medical staff.

Somehow, I managed to get myself invited to the monthly surgeons' meeting, where I politely asked about the reasons for the two-night policy. The first was that 'Older folks on their own sometimes stuff up the bowel prep, and we can't do the procedure with bowels full of faecal matter.' The second night had been instituted many years before because someone had a haemorrhage at home alone, and nearly died before they were discovered. I asked what they would think about us providing a trained community worker to spend a few hours with their patients on each of the two nights. The chief surgeon cut short discussion and said, 'Sounds like a bloody good idea, and I'm all for it unless any of you have any objections.' All heads nodded, and that was that. Within a couple of weeks, the ward was empty. With one short discussion, hundreds of people each year would not be going to stay in hospital for a colonoscopy. The cost to ACCA? $200 to -$300 per patient.

Parklands stand-off

One evening, our call centre was contacted by a policeman about a 'current situation that's going pear-shaped'. A young woman lived in a small van, usually parking in the west parklands at night, driving in to the city each day for a wash and meals. Right now, she was in a tense stand-off with a police patrol. She and her dog, a Doberman, had returned from a walk to find the van's windscreen smashed. She became mentally unwell very quickly, screaming at passers-by, accusing them of doing it, which soon resulted in a triple-0 call that brought the police. They were confronted by an obviously psychotic person, being fiercely protected by a large dog. Plan A was to separate her from the dog (it was going to be messy) and take her to an emergency department for a psychiatric assessment. The police call centre people agreed with their plan, because she was a 'well-known mental patient' who had been in secure care several times in the last couple of years, with a total of more than a hundred nights in hospital.

Amazingly, the policeman thought of us in that moment (maybe it was worrying about how to control the dog) and rang to see if we had any other ideas. He said he thought the big problem was her fear of sleeping in the van with no windscreen. We asked him if it would help if we replaced the windscreen. He liked the idea as long as it could happen quickly. It took an hour and the job was done. The woman and her dog drove off in the van, and the police patrol left for another call. The total cost to ACCA? $244 for the windscreen. In a lovely postscript, the next day the manager of Windscreens O'Brien called to ask if the woman was OK, and to say he was reducing the amount owed to cost-price only. Turns out there was serious mental illness in his own family, and he was happy to have been able to play his part in getting this woman out of a crisis; one he knew all too well could have ended very badly. Even if Plan A had gone reasonably smoothly, the woman would have been in hospital again, terribly distressed, probably for a long stay, her choice of lifestyle ruined.

Door locks

A senior nurse from a large psychiatric ward in a teaching hospital asked us to visit to discuss a bed-blocker who had been there for about thirty-five nights. She came in as a voluntary patient, during a period of mania due to her bipolar disorder. A change of medication had calmed her down, but she had remained highly anxious about going home, because she believed that people had broken in and changed the locks. Stronger antipsychotic medication combined with individual and group therapy had not shaken this belief, so every time they suggested she go home, she became hysterical. The hospital administration was now breathing down their necks about the back-up of people in other wards and the emergency department, needing a bed in the psych ward. In desperation, they called us.

We sent in a nurse who sat with the woman, and asked what we could do to help. She asked us to get her locks changed. We did, at a cost of about $150, and went in the next day to tell her it was done. She asked us to accompany her to her home when she left the hospital that day, so that she could check the locks with us there. We did that, all was OK, she thanked us and told us we could leave.

Of course, there were many times we just couldn't make any headway, even though we knew community care would be effective and preferable to the individual and their family. Such as when respiratory surgeons insisted that children with cystic fibrosis come into hospital for every appointment, when the wider trend was to keep people with such compromised resistance to all sorts of infections as far away from hospital as possible. Why? Because they didn't trust GPs. No discussion about this was even countenanced.

But with such a huge number of people we could help, with full cooperation from the person themselves, their GP and all other clinicians involved, we learned to be patient, and not use up much energy on the ones we couldn't win. Every hospital, every GP was different, and often the right mix of people would coalesce out of the blue, enabling the previously unthinkable to become what everyone wanted.

We had absorbed some key lessons from all this.

First, most of the reasons for unnecessary hospital visits or long stays were not clinical. They were social and psychological. The majority of our interventions were about companionship, practical help with food, transport and negotiating new options in the community. It rankled many health bureaucrats and professionals, but this was just as much about welfare work as it was about new ways of delivering clinical services.

Second, people didn't need to be assessed, reassessed and reassessed every time they needed help. Almost all our clients had extensive records in the health system, and we almost never started a new investigation.

That took time, and if decisions about alternatives were not made immediately, hospital was the default. We used the information that was already available, because there was usually more than enough.

Third, we had the right mantra: 'whatever it takes'. We gave our people the mandate and the means to follow their nose to quickly available solutions, doing things that were just not possible for clinicians in any setting. Usual practice in health systems, then and now, simply doesn't have all the answers.

After a little more than three years, the government contracts for all this work – by then worth about $7 million a year – were put out for tender. ACCA was on course to provide 22,000 episodes of care that year. But we lost the lot to a for-profit nurse-run company that ignored all three of the lessons above. The delays, unnecessary costs and narrowly clinical understandings were back, and the impact was quickly obvious.

The consultant in charge of one emergency department lamented to me a few months later, 'David, the wrinklies and psychos are back, and the ambulance gridlocks are back and what the hell was the Department of Health thinking?'

It was hard for me for a while. I suppose it dented my faith in progress. Things don't always lean towards gradual improvement. This was some of the most satisfying work I'd ever been involved in, in terms of giving people a better health service. But health tribalism, clumsy bureaucracy and some silly interpersonal issues between key players undid most of our work overnight. More than ten years later, I have to admit it still grieves me to think of how all that ended. There are parts of the world – Canada and New Zealand are leading examples – where the lessons we learned underpin widely accepted policy and practice. In Australia, community programs that provide alternatives to unnecessary hospitalisation are still growing painfully slowly; front and centre in every policy document, but usually lucky if they get the small change left over from running hospitals. The tipping point will come eventually, but the age of hospital dominance of Australian health systems has many years to go yet.

My Focus Is Mental Illness

In 2004, I became a board member of the Mental Illness Fellowship of Australia (MIFA), a national federation of community-based NGOs. Their board chairs and CEOs were a great bunch of people with a common objective – better services and community acceptance for people with mental illness anywhere in Australia. It had been more than ten years since I was bundled out of leading mental health reforms in South Australia, but the juice still ran strongly in me on this one. It was unfinished business, and probably always will be.

In 2009, the national CEO of MIFA was rocked by the suicide of her son, who had finally given up the struggle against the ravages of schizophrenia. He had been remarkably well for a time, but the early warning signs were there; he knew another episode was on the way. It was too much to bear. He told her he loved her then went for a walk and jumped off a building. Margaret, working in the garden, stopped to think about the way he had spoken to her, suddenly realising it sounded like a farewell. He had mentioned the tall office block near her house before, so she hurried there. She found him, and was alone with his broken body until the ambulance arrived. She told me she will always be grateful she had that opportunity to say goodbye in private. Although she handled the aftermath brilliantly, Margaret decided to take a back seat for a while, and resigned.

Which left MIFA looking for a CEO. Apart from being a member of the MIFA and two other boards, I was busy earning a living with two jobs, one as CEO of a small privately owned health company, and one working around Australia and New Zealand as a consultant. But I knew a day job at MIFA was the ideal place for me. It was a national role, and I had always wanted to work at that level. It was smack in the centre of my main passion, and I knew there was so much that could be achieved if I kept the job for a few years. It meant getting the best out of a consortium of partner organisations, the sort of work I had done several times before. And it involved a lot of travelling, which I have always loved. With Charmaine's and my kids all largely independent, this was the time to take off to all parts of Australia; a chance to make a real difference.

There was a money problem: MIFA had a tiny budget. I offered to start on three days a week, at a very low rate, banking on continued consulting work for the rest of my income. With a partner who was a senior academic, and a small pension from my public servant days, we didn't need much money anyway, which was a freedom to be enjoyed. The MIFA board agreed within a few days, and I started in a role that turned out to be a perfect fit for me, better even than I had hoped for.

First, I needed an offsider. Susan had worked with me several times in the previous ten years, but she was currently based in Cairns. One phone call and we were a team again, her also part-time but not fussed about it. She was a savant of information, and what she didn't know she could dig up faster than anyone. A genius, who could digest a two-hundred-page government report in a couple of hours, and give me the only things that mattered, in a dot-point summary that I could trust completely. And a no-nonsense woman with a sharp tongue who kept me grounded whenever I showed any signs of self-importance. Whatever I achieved in that job, she was half of it, but she absolutely refused to share the limelight. When it came time for her farewell a few years later, I asked her if she would make a little speech. She snapped back, 'I'd rather stick a fork in my eye.' We worked so well together; I'm missing those days with Susan keenly as I write this.

Our job was to keep the impacts of severe mental illness on the radar across Australia, and to influence policy and funding decisions wherever we could. Margaret had given me a legacy of many opened doors in Canberra, the national capital, and I worked hard to build on what she had started. I particularly liked the Parliamentary Friends of Mental Illness that she had invented, and so did a couple of pharmaceutical companies who funded it generously. That became a vehicle to get people who were dealing with severe illnesses telling their story directly to politicians, their staff and bureaucrats. Choosing the best speakers there became our art form, because getting it right meant huge impact with the real decision-makers. Here are two examples.

The most dangerous woman

Janet is a well-known activist in mental health circles in Australia, and has been for close to forty years. Although she is hugely respected, she can scare the daylights out of people she disagrees with; famous for some blunt, public put-downs of fellow-activists, senior bureaucrats and government ministers alike. So I take it a sort of badge of honour that she appears to consider me an honourable and sensible person, most of the time at least.

While living in a convent as a nun, in her early twenties Janet had her first psychotic episode. For the next fifteen years, she spent more time in secure mental hospital wards than anywhere else. Her schizophrenia was almost unremittingly severe, and she became known as the most dangerous female patient in the New South Wales system. In the notorious Gladesville Hospital, for most of the 1970s she endured 'Horrendous abuse, emotional abuse, physical abuse and sexual abuse – years later when I contacted as many people as I could that I knew had been there and I only ever met one who hadn't been sexually abused.' ('All in the mind' interview, ABC Radio, 10 December 2017)

Janet described to me the moment she began to believe there might be a way out of this. A nurse gave her a remarkable chance, by taking her to his family home at Christmas time, without telling his superiors. She was allowed to hold his newborn baby throughout the evening. One person treating her as an equal, and risking his job to do it, was her turning point.

In 2015, after some debate, Janet agreed to come with me to

Parliament House in Canberra, to be the guest speaker at an event I had organised. We sat together as social chatter over breakfast went on between politicians from all parties and their chiefs of staff, some senior bureaucrats, drug company representatives and a few of my national advocacy colleagues. She was very tense, and whispered to me that she was going to say things she had never said in public before. Was I sure it was the right thing to do? I told her it was essential information for these people to hear first-hand, if she was up to it. I did the usual introduction, mentioning her AM award in the Australian honours system, and her appointment as a commissioner in the recently established National Mental Health Commission. She stood at the microphone, not speaking for a few seconds, looking into the middle distance, and now it was my turn to be tense. She breathed in, and started talking.

For the next twenty minutes, there was no sound except her voice. A quiet, clear voice saying horrifying, scary, sad and also very funny things. All clatter of plates and cutlery stopped. Food halfway to mouths stayed there going cold. I watched faces, and saw tears, hands at mouths, deep breaths being taken, heads shaking and everywhere, utter absorption, even among the serving staff. When she finished, there was an eruption of emotional applause. In my job, this was the sort of impact on funders and policy makers that really changes the conversation. A woman who could have been your sister or mother, who had come back from hell to let us know we had to do better in future.

The first question was 'Do you still hear voices?'

She looked at me, and after a few moments' hesitation said, 'All the time – it's happening now. A voice just told me not to be so fucking stupid talking to you lot about this. Of course, we people who hear voices rarely say this, because you all get so anxious about it. We usually lie even to our psychiatrists about it, because they just want to increase or change your medication. And most of us know better than they do what medication and in what dose works best for us. I've had fifty years of practice with that one. I don't like being this fat, but for me, olanzapine, with its well-known weight gain side effects, is an old and trusted friend, so I'm prepared to put up with not having a girlish figure.'

As the breakfast broke up, staff and politicians all going to their frantic rounds of sittings and meetings, people queued up to shake Janet's hand. Emotions were still high. It is people like Janet that really change minds and open hearts. Afterwards she asked me if she had made any sense. I just hugged her.

The expert

Another speaker was a middle-aged mother, whose son had paranoid schizophrenia. I think it was Carers Week, which was a good opportunity to get the attention of politicians, particularly to sensitise them to the load that families carry when one or more members are coping with mental illness.

She talked about her son, how he had been top of his class in school, great at sports, and an outgoing, personable young man. In first-year university, it all went pear-shaped when, apparently without warning, he became psychotic, an episode that lasted for many months while he was in hospital care. I say 'apparently', because many people begin to remember that things had begun to change a bit earlier, sometimes years earlier, but put that down to the usual turbulence of adolescence. And it's true – most boys who shut themselves in their room and play loud music with dark lyrics do not have mental illness.

Anyway, her boy did, and when he came home from hospital, quiet, getting fat, uninterested in any daily activities and 'talking a bit weird', she had to think long and hard about how to do this. A single mother, with a reasonable income, she decided that her dearest love, her only child, would never be thrown out of his home, no matter what. That commitment was to be severely, and repeatedly, tested.

Her son began to get into trouble with local people, first by talking loudly to himself in shops, then by abusing a neighbour he believed was spying on him. The police were called to the house several times, and his voices began to tell him that his mother was plotting to have him locked up for ever. Luckily, she had access to a carer support and education program, and had learned a bit about psychosis, what is happening, what to expect, and how to communicate with a person hearing voices.

Matters came to a head when he came into the kitchen one afternoon, got a large knife from a drawer, and told her that she had to stop scheming against him, or he might have to kill her. He told her this while cornering her by the refrigerator, with the knife pointing at her stomach.

She said roughly this, 'You and I both know that the voices are not you. I know some of them are very important to you, but they are not the core of you. You and I are always going to be together because we love each other. So maybe the voices have got a bit mixed up on this one. You know in your heart I will never hurt you, and you could never hurt me. Now, I know how hard it is for you to concentrate with the voices all talking at once, but I've seen you do it. I'm going to go for a walk around the block, and I'll be back in about twenty minutes. In that time, just try to calm down and think about the lovely tea we are going to have together, before we watch the news and then maybe try a crossword. Can you do that?'

He backed away, and she walked slowly out of the room, her back feeling like the easiest of targets, Outside, shaking, she briefly considered calling the police, then decided this was her life to manage, whatever the risks.

Twenty minutes later, breathing a bit more easily, she came back to find him sitting quietly in the lounge room. She walked over, kissed him on the head and said, 'I love you.'

He said, 'I love you too, Mum. Can we have tea now?'

She excused herself to have a shower, where she sobbed for a while, then they had tea together.

While she had been speaking, I was sitting next to a cabinet minister in a conservative government, a curious blend of a man who was both a right-wing hard enforcer, and someone who had recently revealed he had been fighting depression for several years.

He turned to me and said, 'You've brought along some interesting speakers to these meetings David, some of them so-called experts. But none of them can hold a candle to the expert we've just listened to.'

I had to connect with the top decision-makers, and I just went for it. I had one-on-one meetings with all the relevant ministers and heads of departments. They usually wanted one-page simplified summaries of issues, giving them a clear path to making a real difference that they could claim the credit for. There's just no point in telling these people how awful it all is, if you can't help them see a way to make a start on doing something useful. I also made sure I praised the good initiatives, and offered to work with them to make sure they were implemented well. Because our member organisations were all well-established, authentic voices of 'lived experience', I went to Canberra loaded with their service medals; accepted as an impartial, honest advisor, with good knowledge of the national picture, and with no axe to grind except helping people in desperate straits.

Not long after I started, the pharmaceutical company that had been giving MIFA about $100,000 a year received legal advice that they were in breach of their new industry code of conduct. By providing such a large proportion of our total income, they might be perceived to have undue influence. They reduced their grant to $10,000. Until that time, the member organisations had only been putting in small amounts, and MIFA now faced being wound up. Now they faced a tough decision: either give a lot more, or give up the game of being a national advocate of any relevance. After very little debate, it was agreed that each member would give a percentage of their annual turnover to MIFA. That gave us a budget of nearly $250,000, which was more than I had suggested, partly because they wanted me to become full-time, at a better rate of pay. I was very happy to agree.

There were difficulties. Within a few months, one member

organisation – as usual in these matters, the largest one – began grumbling about the value they got from meeting their share of the cost. They worried that they might have been hasty in not thinking through their capacity to lobby government on their own, without depending on a national body. In Australian federated bodies, these spats always seem to originate with tensions between the Victorian and the New South Wales people, and this one was no exception. With frequent visits to our Victorian member's board meetings in Melbourne, I managed to keep them at the table for a year, but it was an increasing distraction from our core business of trying to make things better for people dealing with mental illness. When most of your debates are about internal politics, and not about your customers, any organisation is in big danger of losing its way. It was a bit bloody when the Victorians left, and it meant I had to spend more time finding other sources of funding, but I was actually relieved when they took their ball and went home. The other members were so pleased to see them go that they further increased their contributions to MIFA to help close the funding gap. Their loyalty to each other, and support to me as CEO, was absolutely solid from then on.

The next couple of years were a buzz. I was invited to help the federal government design a new initiative that received about $500 million funding over four years. It laboured under a clumsy name something like 'A federal program of coordinated care for people with severe and persistent mental illness', which luckily morphed into Partners in Recovery. That program has been an outstanding success, helping thousands of hard-to-reach people who can't or won't engage with what's on offer. People living under bridges. People in jail. People hidden in family homes where parents consumed by shame had no idea what to do about their child's relentless downward spiral. Partners in Recovery reached out to these people in ways that had never been possible before, and everyone from psychiatrists to general practitioners and police loved it.

MIFA also continued to be influential in the expansion of other federal and state programs that supported families doing it tough with dads, mums, sons and daughters with severe mental illness. The federal minister at the time, Mark Butler, fully endorsed modern understandings of the types of supports needed, and I had excellent access to both him and his advisors. He made a number of visits to locations run by MIFA members in every state, organised through my office. He was happy to recognise us as the group with genuine grass-roots support across Australia.

These halcyon days never last, and the power cut that nearly switched out our lights came in the form of the National Disability Insurance Scheme. During 2012, I was a member of an expert advisory committee, looking at how the proposed model could work for people with 'psychosocial disability' affecting people with the most severe and persistent severe mental illness. It seemed too good to be true – an extra $1.2 billion for our people each year from about 2016 onwards. How could we say no? I was warned by a colleague on the committee, 'We aren't really having any influence, David. We're just salad dressing on a meal being cooked up somewhere else.' He was so right.

Several months after the committee finished and reported, a senior bureaucrat in Canberra took me aside to tell me the exciting news. The NDIS was going ahead, the legislation would be in Parliament within weeks, and trial sites in two states would start within a few months. I asked how it would be paid for. The answer was 'No problems. We can put in about half the money by closing down current state and federally funded programs for people who need this most, and the rest of the money will come from an increase in the Medicare levy.' I asked which programs would close down. It was all the services we had been building for the last ten years, including Partners in Recovery. I was gobsmacked.

'But the NDIS is only for 65,000 people, the most severely and persistently and permanently disabled, right? What about the other 200,000 or more Australians only slightly less disabled, who can access all the current programs? They won't get into the NDIS and their current services will disappear. We all agreed the NDIS would be great as an addition to the options available, but now you're saying it's an alternative, for about a quarter of them, and the rest get nothing?'

The answer was, 'We don't agree with those figures, David. In any case, the other groups you mentioned shouldn't have been in these programs anyway, and the states and territories will need to step up and meet their needs.'

And there you have it. That conversation was in March 2013, and the rationale was pure fiction; part of a mad scramble by a government under extreme pressure to find a way to prove that Australia could afford the NDIS. But the legislation went ahead unchallenged, and five years later, individuals and families are finding doors closing that used to be open, staff are being sacked in large numbers, and state and federal governments are still not really admitting they made a huge error of judgement in 2013. Belatedly agreeing to some extent, but too little and too late for so many people in need, and for the mental health workers who wanted to walk alongside them.

From that time in 2013 to when I retired at the end of 2016, most of my job became trying to hold the line, persuading as many decision-makers and other people with a voice in the game as I could to call it out: governments of all parties had no mandate to desert these people, and talking rubbish about Australia making great strides with mental health could not be excused just because a minority were going to get a better deal sometime soon. We made submissions to parliamentary committees, we spoke to newspapers, we presented papers at conferences, while all the time trying to cooperate constructively where the scheme was slowly rolling out to provide new life opportunities to a small number of the right people. I and a few others on the case made some headway; delaying transfer of funding to the scheme by a couple of years at least, convincing the federal government to allocate much more 'transition' funding, and several states and territories to plug gaps as they showed up.

I never quite got over the feeling that we did far too little in 2013 when the problem emerged. Like most people, I couldn't believe the government was serious about closing down programs like Partners in Recovery – programs they had boldly announced and funded only two years before; programs that were universally popular, and undoubtedly turned around many lives blighted by mental illness. While we dithered trying to understand how it might play out, the legislation went through, and then it was all too late. Having said that, from then on we decided to 'give 'em hell' every chance we got, to keep on pointing out the truth and the possible ways out of the impasse that was approaching.

It's hard to rail against the machine when governments of both major parties have decided to implement a $22 billion scheme. The PR was relentless, and it included painting critics like us as self-serving, and/or ignorant of the facts, and/or too risk-averse to see a wonderful opportunity ahead. But we knew we were fighting for the future of the people we cared about, so I had to learn some new behaviours. I've always wondered at the ability of legal, industrial and political professionals to keep on repeating the same arguments, in the same words, at every chance they get. I get so bored with the sound of my own voice repeating itself. I think that has something to do with my lifelong pattern of changing jobs every few years. Anyway, it hit me that I had to accept the role of inflexible standard-bearer and do it very well; it was what they paid me for.

For three years, I became a one-note warrior, turning up wherever I could to explain for the umpteenth time that the NDIS was a great concept for those few who would get into it, but everybody else dealing with serious mental illness had to join the fight to maintain vital services. I averaged eighty trips a year during that time, and there were days when I felt like George Clooney in the film *Up in the Air*, when he's asked by the pilot where he lives. 'Here,' says George, pointing to his seat in the plane. I started thinking about my pitch for the next speaking engagement when I was eating breakfast; I was still thinking about it watching TV that night, and then I even dreamed about it.

Where was the clincher, the cut-through lines and pictures that would sway the NDIS zealots? Or at least get them to agree we needed a Plan B for people who would miss out on the NDIS?

As always, during those intense, heady days, it was real people living with the impacts of mental illness that kept me grounded – even when I was up in a plane. I got to meet some amazing people, who shared their stories with generosity and bravery. Here's just one.

The nail technician

We were all getting grumpy. The plane had been sitting on the tarmac at Townsville for about fifteen minutes, since the captain had announced we were still waiting for one passenger to board. Then there was a very glamorous woman in the aisle, apologising loudly, flashing a huge smile and much else as she sashayed towards me. Two big shopping bags, loads of bling and dramatically high heels; no one could resist staring as she checked the seat numbers. Then she was standing right there, asking if I would mind letting her get into the window seat, and would I help her put her heavy bags in the luggage lockers above us.

For ten minutes or so, as we taxied and took off, I continued with the games in the Qantas magazine. Sudoku conquered, I glanced over to see that she had the most preposterously elaborate fingernail decorations, green and three-dimensional, like tiny cream cakes on each nail, topped with glitter. I asked her how she kept them from being damaged, and she said they would be unlikely to survive more than a few hours, which was partly why she wanted my help stowing the bags. So why? She had been the lead judge at the nail technician of the year finals for north Queensland, and had volunteered to be the model for one of the contestants. This over-the-top adornment was in fact the winning entry.

OK I confess. I hadn't expected a riveting conversation, but I was wrong. She had a very successful business on the Gold Coast, and worked as a visiting expert in other salons, hiring herself out at $180 an hour. Her business savvy was obviously impressive, she lectured and demonstrated her craft across Australia and she was the reigning president of the relevant professional body in Queensland. She owned her own home, and had a bought a house for her mother. And she hadn't even finished high school.

Then she asked me about my job. I told her about doing my bit round the country to improve services and build community understanding and acceptance that mental illness is everybody's business. She listened very quietly.

After a while, she asked me to move so she could go to the toilet. When she returned, she sat looking out the window for a few minutes, until the staff brought us a snack and drink. I turned to find her looking at me intently, and I noticed beads of sweat above her lips. She was clearly very tense about something.

As soon as the cabin staff had left she said, 'My mother has schizophrenia. I've been looking after her since I was eight years old.' A few words for a world of hurt. A few words to remind me yet again not to make assumptions

At eight, her father disappeared. Her mum had been admitted to the local mental hospital several times after suicide attempts by then, and now this girl in year three primary school had to take over. With a much younger brother to look after, as well as a mum who could barely get out of bed most days, she often got to school late, but her mum made her promise not to say why, 'Or else the welfare will put you and your brother in a home, and lock me up.' All through her school years she was afraid every day; that her Mum would kill herself; that her little brother wasn't safe; that she would fall so far behind in school that she would never be able to get a job; and worst, that someone would find out about her mum.

When she was about fifteen, someone did report the family to the welfare department. Luckily, a recently established community mental health program on the Gold Coast decided to help her keep the family together. In her last year of high school, at last she could go to school knowing that a support worker would visit her mum, and a family day care family would look after her brother until she picked him up after school. With that support, she got to the school leaving age, then decided to go to work.

Now at thirty-four, she was at the top of her profession, and financially secure. As community programs came and went, she had found herself having to renegotiate home care and accommodation for her mother time and again, until she decided she would pay for it all herself. She bought a small house near her own home, gave it to her mother, and paid for a care worker to visit every weekday. Her mother's mental health was not improving, and her physical health was deteriorating rapidly, but 'I'm going to be there for Mum for as long as she needs me.'

The plane landed, and I helped her get her bags down.

She said, 'Thanks for that.' and began an exit just as dramatic as her entrance.

I looked around and saw every male and many female eyes following her. I wanted to tell them all, 'She's so much more than you're thinking.'

Unfortunately, every time I got off a plane, it was to be confronted by the NDIS. Like a slow-moving steamroller, it ground on towards us, and it became achingly obvious that we could be absolutely right and still lose. In a Senate inquiry, I watched a very senior bureaucrat talking rubbish about there being 'no disadvantage to any existing clients'; rubbish that I and another speaker demolished a few minutes later. I could see all the senators agreed with us, and that's what their report said, but nobody in government appeared to take any notice. Over time, though, as the number of influential people that we persuaded grew, the focus did begin to shift. Queensland and the Northern Territory lead the way with new funding for people not eligible for the NDIS. Forums that MIFA people initiated were attended by their key decision-makers. These days, only a few NDIS spin-merchants would have a hide thick enough to parrot the 'no disadvantage' clichés. The real debates for the last couple of years have been about how to find new funding to cover the looming gaps.

Retirement

I had to retire sometime, and at seventy there were other adventures I didn't want to miss out on. A year living in Bali beckoned to Charmaine and me, so at the end of 2016 I pulled the plug. I had several farewells, which touched me deeply. Staying much longer in this role – seven years – than any job I had done for nearly thirty years brought many pleasures; good friendships that will last, a sense of some solid achievements, and not least, great farewell parties, overflowing with mutual and genuine appreciation.

In my last week on the job, I went to a forum in Canberra. I looked around the room at people from all over Australia that I knew now, colleagues I had such respect for, and listened to several bureaucrats giving a tired, largely misleading analysis of why we were all needlessly worried about the NDIS. I finished with a flourish, telling them they were trying to rewrite history, and that nobody believed a word of it. I confess, it was delicious fun, and the applause was nice. When it was over, I sat there feeling very sad, watching people planning their next trip, conference, newspaper interview et cetera, hoping I had made the right decision.

A woman I'd never met sat down beside me. She said, 'You're the only one here today who talked sense. We're going to miss you.'

OK, we had a long way to go to win this huge struggle to maintain good services for people with mental illness, but for me, at that moment, it was a perfect ending.

It's a couple of years since then, and my successor is doing a great job. He's at all the 'top tables' and has the ear of key government ministers of health and social services. The 'valley of death' scenario, with new NDIS funding coming too late to keep existing staff and services going, has hit hard. Hundreds of mental health workers have been sacked, and the majority of the people they were helping have been left to fend for themselves. I think the worst is over, and I frequently hear about new initiatives emerging around Australia; 'green shoots' is the current management-speak. I think the NDIS is being implemented with breathtaking clumsiness and constant delays, but several thousand people around the country are getting the real 'choice and control' over the new and generously funded NDIS packages of care that they were promised.

In retirement, I have a very minor role, as a member of three boards, and as a community visitor volunteer. These day,s my thoughts are just as often with a project I'm involved with in Bali. Yes, it's about helping people affected by serious mental illness. Perhaps an episode from last year, when we were living in Ubud in Bali, will explain what drives me on this one.

One of the pleasures of living in Ubud is the Saturday quiz night. Expats from many countries (no locals – they scratch their heads at the whole trivia games concept) come together in a café for a couple of hours. The language is English, but much conversation goes on in Dutch, Spanish and German as questions are clarified. Recently, as the quiz was beginning, a young woman wandered in, alone, to our part of the restaurant. She was talking, apparently to no one in particular at first, but then asking loudly what was going on. Several quiz participants called out for her to leave, then some stepped up to her and spoke to her directly. One held her arm as if to lead her away. I noticed the *pecalang* (local volunteer police) moving into the area behind us, and the tension was ramping rapidly. All chatting stopped as people looked on.

It hit me then that she might be psychotic, hearing one or more voices and not able to work out what was being asked of her. I went to her and asked everyone else to stop talking and step back. I asked her if she could hear me. At first, I couldn't get eye contact, but when that happened, she looked at me for a long five seconds or so, then said, 'Yes I can hear you.' As the others returned to their seats, I explained to her that this was a private party, a quiz night, and that she was welcome to be in the rest of the restaurant but not here. She responded, 'So, OK it's private, but could I please just stay here and listen?' I showed her a chair where she could sit as long as she was just going to listen. She sat down.

My attention had been completely on this interaction, and I was reasonably happy with the outcome. But as I turned around, I saw two things immediately. First was a sea of quiz participants' faces all registering negatives – some concern, fear and confusion, but mostly people being pissed off at this young woman. The quizmaster looked particularly angry. Second, behind the quiz area, there were now four *pecalang* and the restaurant manager closing in, looking to evict her. I went to them quickly and said things should be OK now, and asked the quizmaster to resume.

For about ten minutes, the quiz went along as usual, then the woman stood up, went to the quizmaster, took his glass of wine and returned to her seat. In the ensuing confusion, I took the glass of wine from her, the quizmaster demanded I get her out of there, and I guided her to the other part of the restaurant. But the *pecalang* pushed me aside, took her by the arms, and frogmarched her off the premises. I went with them as far as the street, trying in my best Indonesian to say this was not necessary, but having no impact. They went away into the darkness, her struggling a little and protesting, and I came back to the quiz, aware of intense scrutiny from my friends. A little hesitantly at first, the quizmaster resumed.

I found it very hard to calm down. I know there is no service available in Ubud for people with mental illness, so I don't know what the *pecalang* might have done next. I was angry at myself for not trying harder to stop this spiral of confusion that ended so badly in forcible restraint. I was thinking this woman was about the same age as my daughter, and how distressed she must be now, and how her parents would have coped if they had seen what happened. I really couldn't have cared less about the quiz questions; what the flag of Libya looked like, or who the prime minister of Sri Lanka was.

That night in bed, I thought about her with rising sadness and some anger. The incident stays with me, despite the nice things a few people said to me afterwards about my actions. It hit me hard that such a cosmopolitan group of Westerners could have so little understanding about what severe mental illness looks like, and that many of them seemed to jump immediately to blaming the victim. I've tried to channel those emotions into working for better mental health services in Bali.

So far, several dozen people, all Balinese living in or near Ubud, have come forward for treatment as a result of a small project I'm involved with. I was lucky enough to find a GP and a psychiatrist who were prepared to offer their services for free. I've also given a presentation to the Ubud Rotary Club about mental illness. The session went very well, and they are supportive now, but I had to get past the callous jokes and ridicule that the topic so often brings out. I'm trying to be positive; to believe there will be a day when someone like that woman will be responded to with compassion and competent care. It's going to be a long haul.

Of course, these challenges don't go away just because some of us change jobs or retire. I had another sharp reminder just a few weeks ago, during a cab ride from Melbourne airport. There are so many taxi driver stories I could tell. Probably more than any other situation, these quiet, intimate conversations convince me that mental illness is virtually every family's business. This particular long, slow trip started with a typical discussion of the impact of Uber on the taxi industry. The driver, a recent migrant from Lebanon (with remarkably good English, and fluent in French and Arabic) explained without complaint how his income had reduced in three years from a net of $70,000 a year to about $45,000. 'Uber will win in the end, and who am I to say that is not better for everybody?'

He had a wife and three children, and I asked how the family got by. It was getting very difficult, since his wife had been forced to give up work a few months before, 'because of a family problem'. Paying bills and the mortgage were a constant struggle.

Then he asked me about my life and work. I was on my way to a board meeting about mental illness policy, and briefly summarised my previous job. As soon as I stopped talking, he said, 'The family problem is that our eldest son has developed schizophrenia. He responds best to my wife, so even though her job had been paying better than the taxi income, we agreed she should stay home to look after him.'

We had reached our destination. We sat and talked for a while, him hoping his wife could find some supports for their son so that she could work part-time, me offering a few suggestions about services I knew of in their part of Melbourne. We shook hands warmly, with strong feelings in the air, and he drove away for another long night shift.

There's so much unmet need in the world, so many issues that make us anxious; you can't tackle all of it. Stay focused, and sometimes just a few people working together can make a big difference. As Margaret Mead said, 'It's the only thing that ever has.'

My focus is mental illness, and so long as I can contribute anything useful, I want to do just that.

www.ingramcontent.com/pod-product-compliance
Lightning Source LLC
Chambersburg PA
CBHW030907080526
44589CB00010B/180